THERE IS NO
MALE AND FEMALE

HARVARD DISSERTATIONS IN RELIGION

Editors

Margaret R. Miles
and
Bernadette J. Brooten

Number 20

There Is No Male and Female:
The Fate of a Dominical Saying
in Paul and Gnosticism

Dennis Ronald MacDonald

THERE IS NO
MALE AND FEMALE

The Fate of a Dominical Saying
in Paul and Gnosticism

Dennis Ronald MacDonald

Fortress Press   Philadelphia

BS
2685.2
.M33
1987

Library of Congress Cataloging-in-Publication Data

MacDonald, Dennis Ronald, 1946–
    There is no male and female.

    (Harvard dissertations in religion ; no. 20)
    Bibliography: p.
    1. Bible. N.T. Galatians III. 27–28—Criticism, interpretation, etc. 2. Jesus Christ—Words—Extra-canonical parallels. 3. Gnostic literature.
4. Gnosticism. 5. Sex—Biblical teaching. 6. Sex role—Biblical teaching. I. Title. II. Series.
BS2685.2.M33 1986   227'.406   86–45200
ISBN 0–8006–7076–0

2546B87   Printed in the United States of America   1–7076

To Diane

CONTENTS

PREFACE

This dissertation was inspired by a gratuitous discovery in the second floor of the Harvard Divinity School library one afternoon in November of 1975. Under the title "There Is No Male and Female: Galatians 3:26–28 and Gnostic Baptismal Tradition" it was accepted by the faculty of Harvard University in April of 1978 and was recommended for publication in the series *Harvard Dissertations in Religion*. Inasmuch as almost nine years have interrupted this recommendation and its eventual publication, I have expanded the original work in order to acknowledge the explosion of documentation on the issues and texts germane to the topic. It also seemed appropriate to make some sections friendly to the reader by translating quotations in foreign languages, bumping esoteric discussions to footnotes, lubricating transitions, and so on. The result is a document longer than the original, but faithful to it in organization, argumentation, and conclusions.

No dissertation—certainly not this one—issues from individual effort. The late Professor George MacRae, my dissertation advisor, provided carefully measured encouragement and immeasurable assistance. The other members of the committee, Professors Paul Hanson, Helmut Koester, and John Strugnell, each offered insights without which this study would be impoverished. To the library staffs at the Harvard Divinity School, Goshen College, and the Iliff School of Theology go plaudits for providing the services needed for this research. John Hollar of Fortress Press steered the dissertation to its most appropriate publishing form, and Joe Snowden at the Harvard Divinity School saw it from manuscript to its present form. Above all I am indebted to Diane Louise Prosser MacDonald for having read a dozen drafts of this work without complaint and with consummate care, theological precision, and uxorial ruthlessness. To her this study is appropriately dedicated, since she has helped me understand sexual equality both existentially and theologically.

ABBREVIATIONS

AB	Anchor Bible
ꜗ *Abot R. Nat.*	ꜗ *Abot Rabbi Nathan*
Acts Andr.	*Acts of Andrew*
Acts Barn.	*Acts of Barnabas*
Acts Thom.	*Acts of Thomas*
ALGHJ	Arbeiten zur Literatur und Geschichte des hellenistischen Judentums
Apoc. Moses	*Apocalypse of Moses*
Asc. Isa.	*Ascension of Isaiah*
ASNU	Acta seminarii neotestamentici upsaliensis
AThANT	Abhandlungen zur Theologie des Alten und Neuen Testaments
ATR	*Anglican Theological Review*
BAG	W. Bauer, W. F. Arndt, and F. W. Gingrich, *Greek-English Lexicon of the New Testament*
2 Bar.	*Apocalypse of Baruch*
Ber.	*Berakot*
BFCTH	Beiträge zur Förderung christlicher Theologie
BG	(Codex) Berolinensis Gnosticus
BJRL	*Bulletin of the John Rylands University Library of Manchester*
BLE	*Bulletin de littérature ecclésiastique*
b. Meg.	*Megilla* (Babylonian Talmud)
b. Menach.	*Menachot* (Babylonian Talmud)
b. Moꜥed Qaṭ.	*Moꜥed Qaṭan* (Babylonian Talmud)
b. Ned.	*Nedarim* (Babylonian Talmud)

BSac	*Bibliotheca Sacra*
BTB	*Biblical Theology Bulletin*
BVC	*Bible et vie chrétienne*
BWANT	Beiträge zur Wissenschaft vom Alten und Neuen Testament
b. Yoma	*Yoma (= Kippurim)* (Babylonian Talmud)
BZ	*Biblische Zeitschrift*
BZNW	Beihefte zur *ZNW*
CBQ	*Catholic Biblical Quarterly*
CBQMS	Catholic Biblical Quarterly—Monograph Series
CD	Cairo (Genizah text of the) Damascus Document
CG	Coptic Gnostic Library
2 Clem.	*2 Clement*
Clem. Al.	Clement of Alexandria
Exc. Theod.	*Excerpta Theodoto*
Paid.	*Paidagogos*
Strom.	*Stromateis*
CNT	Commentaire du Nouveau Testament
CSCO	Corpus scriptorum christianorum orientalium
Deut. Rab.	*Deuteronomy Rabbah*
Dial. Sav.	*Dialogue of the Savior*
EKKNT	Evangelisch-katholischer Kommentar zum Neuen Testament
Ep. Barn.	*Epistle of Barnabas*
Epiph.	Epiphanius
Pan.	*Panarion*
Ep. Pet. Phil.	*Letter of Peter to Philip*
ÉThR	*Études théologiques et religieuses*
Eus.	Eusebius
Hist. eccl.	*Historia ecclesiasticae*
EvTh	*Evangelische Theologie*
Exeg. Soul	*Exegesis on the Soul*
Exod. Rab.	*Exodus Rabbah*
ExpTim	*Expository Times*
FBBS	Facet Books, Biblical Series
FRLANT	Forschungen zur Religion und Literatur des Alten und Neuen Testaments
GCS	Griechische christliche Schriftsteller
Gen. Rab.	*Genesis Rabbah*
Giṭ.	*Giṭṭin*
Gos. Eg.	*Gospel of the Egyptians*
Gos. Phil.	*Gospel of Philip*

Gos. Thom.	*Gospel of Thomas*
Herm. Sim.	*Hermas, Similitude*
Hippol.	Hippolytus
Haer.	*Refutatio omnium haeresium*
HNT	Handbuch zum Neuen Testament
HR	*History of Religions*
HThKNT	Herders theologischer Kommentar zum Neuen Testament
HTR	*Harvard Theological Review*
IB	*Interpreter's Bible*
ICC	International Critical Commentary
Iren.	Irenaeus
Adv. haer.	*Adversus haereses*
JAAR	*Journal of the American Academy of Religion*
JBL	*Journal of Biblical Literature*
JETS	*Journal of the Evangelical Theological Society*
JSNT	*Journal for the Study of the New Testament*
JTS	*Journal of Theological Studies*
Justin	
1 Apol.	*First Apology*
KD	*Kerygma und Dogma*
LCL	Loeb Classical Library
LSJ	Liddell-Scott-Jones, *Greek-English Lexicon*
Mek.	*Mekilta*
MeyerK	H. A. W. Meyer, Kritisch-exegetischer Kommentar über das Neue Testament
m. Ketub.	*Ketubot* (Mishnah)
MNTC	Moffat NT Commentary
NHC	Nag Hammadi Codices
NHS	Nag Hammadi Studies
NICNT	New International Commentary on the New Testament
NKZ	*Neue kirchliche Zeitschrift*
NovT	*Novum Testamentum*
NovTSup	*Novum Testamentum*, Supplements
NRTh	*La nouvelle revue théologique*
NTAbh	Neutestamentliche Abhandlungen
NTApoc	Hennecke-Schneemelcher, *New Testament Apocrypha*
NTS	*New Testament Studies*
NumenSup	*Numen: International Review for the History of Religions*, Supplements
Num. Rab.	*Numbers Rabbah*

Odes Sol.	*Odes of Solomon*
OrChrA	Orientalia Christiana Analecta
Origen	
Cels.	*Contra Celsum*
Ox. Pap.	Oxyrhynchus Papyrus
PG	J. Migne, *Patrologia graeca*
Philo of Alexandria	
De agric.	*De agricultura*
De cher.	*De cherubim*
De conf.	*De confusione linguarum*
De fuga	*De fuga et inventione*
De gig.	*De gigantibus*
De mig.	*De migratione Abrahami*
De Mos.	*De vita Mosis*
De mut. nom.	*De mutatione nominum*
De op. mun.	*De opificio mundi*
De plant.	*De plantatione*
De post. Caini	*De posteritate Caini*
De praem.	*De praemiis et poenis*
De sac.	*De sacrificiis Abelis et Caini*
De som.	*De somniis*
De spec. leg.	*De specialibus legibus*
De virt.	*De virtutibus*
De vita cont.	*De vita contemplativa*
Leg. all.	*Legum allegoriarum*
Quest. Gen.	*Questiones et solutiones in Genesim*
Quis her.	*Quis rerum divinarum heres sit*
Quod. det.	*Quod deterius potiori insidiari soleat*
Quod Deus imm.	*Quod Deus sit immutabilis*
Quod prob.	*Quod omnis probus liber sit*
Pirqe R. El.	*Pirqe Rabbi Eliezer*
PL	J. Migne, *Patrologia latina*
Ps.-Cl.	*Pseudo-Clementines*
Hom.	*Homilies*
Recog.	*Recognitions*
1QS	*Rule of the Community, Manual of Discipline*
RB	*Revue biblique*
RevistB	*Revista biblica*
RHPhR	*Revue d'histoire et de philosophie religieuses*
RThL	*Revue théologique de Louvain*
RThPh	*Revue de théologie et de philosophie*

SBLDS	Society of Biblical Literature Dissertation Series
SBT	Studies in Biblical Theology
Sipre Num.	*Sipre Numbers*
Soph. Jes. Chr.	*Sophia of Jesus Christ*
StPatr	*Studia Patristica* I–XIV (=TU 63–64 [1957], 78–79 [1961], 80–81 [1962], 92–94 [1966], 115–16 [1975], 117 [1976])
Str-B	[H. Strack and] Paul Billerbeck, *Kommentar zum Neuen Testament*
t. Ber.	*Berakot* (Tosephta)
TDNT	G. Kittel and G. Friedrich (eds.), *Theological Dictionary of the New Testament*
Tert.	Tertullian
Adv. Marc.	*Adversus Marcionem*
Adv. Val.	*Adversus Valentinum*
De praesc. haer.	*De praescriptione haereticorum*
Res. carn.	*De resurrectione carnis*
Tg. Onq.	*Targum Onqelos*
ThH	*Théologie Historique*
ThHKNT	Theologischer Handkommentar zum Neuen Testament
Thom. Cont.	*Book of Thomas the Contender*
ThQ	*Theologische Quartalschrift*
Treat. Res.	*Treatise on Resurrection*
Tri. Trac.	*Tripartite Tractate*
TS	*Theological Studies*
t. Soṭa	*Soṭa* (Tosephta)
TToday	*Theology Today*
TU	Texte und Untersuchungen
VC	*Vigiliae christianae*
WTJ	*Westminster Theological Journal*
WUNT	Wissenschaftliche Untersuchungen zum Neuen Testament
y. Ber.	*Berakot* (Jerusalem Talmud)
ZKG	*Zeitschrift für Kirchengeschichte*
ZNW	*Zeitschrift für die neutestamentliche Wissenschaft*
ZThK	*Zeitschrift für Theologie und Kirche*

SHORT TITLES

Information appears here for frequently used works which are cited by short title. A few short titles do not appear in this list, but in each instance full bibliography is given on the page(s) preceding such references.

Adinolfi, "Il velo della donna"
> Adinolfi, Marco, "Il velo della donna e la rilettura paolina di 1 Cor. 11,2–16," *RevistBib* 23 (1975) 147–73.

Allo, *Saint Paul*
> Allo, E.-B., *Saint Paul: Première épitre aux Corinthiens* (2d ed.; Paris: Librairie Lecoffre, 1956).

Bachmann, *Der erste Briefe*
> Bachmann, Philipp, *Der erste Briefe des Paulus an die Korinther* (Kommentar zum Neuen Testament 7; Leipzig: Deichert, 1905).

Barrett, *First Epistle*
> Barrett, C. K., *The First Epistle of St Paul to the Corinthians* (New York: Harper & Row, 1968).

Baumann, *Das doppelte Geschlecht*
> Baumann, Hermann, *Das doppelte Geschlecht. Ethnologische Studien zur Bisexualität in Ritus und Mythos* (2d ed.; Berlin: Reimer, 1980).

Betz, *Galatians*
> Betz, Hans Dieter, *Galatians: A Commentary on Paul's Letter to the Churches in Galatia* (Hermeneia; Philadelphia: Fortress, 1979).

Bornhaüser, "'Um der Engel willen'"
> Bornhaüser, D., "'Um der Engel willen.' 1 Kor. 11,10," *NKZ* 41 (1930) 475–88.

Bouttier, "*Complexio Oppositorum*"
> Bouttier, Michel, "*Complexio Oppositorum*: sur les formules de I Cor. XII. 13; Gal. III. 26–28; Col. III. 10, 11," *NTS* 23 (1976) 1–19.

Brinsmead, *Galatians—Dialogical Response to Opponents*
> Brinsmead, Bernard H., *Galatians—Dialogical Response to Opponents* (SBLDS 65; Chico: Scholars Press, 1982).

Broudéhoux, *Mariage et famille*
> Broudéhoux, Jean-Paul, *Mariage et famille chez Clément d'Alexandrie* (*ThH* 2; Paris: Beauchesne, 1970).

Bruce, *1 and 2 Corinthians*
> Bruce, F. F., *1 and 2 Corinthians* (New Century Bible; Greenwood, SC: Attic, 1978).

Brun, "'Um der Engel willen'"
> Brun, Lyder, "'Um der Engel willen' 1 Kor 11,10," *ZNW* 14 (1913) 298–308.

Clark, *Man and Woman in Christ*
> Clark, Stephen B., *Man and Woman in Christ: An Examination of the Roles of Men and Women in Light of Scripture and the Social Sciences* (Ann Arbor: Servant Books, 1980).

Conzelmann, *1 Corinthians*
> Conzelmann, Hans, *1 Corinthians* (Hermeneia; Philadelphia: Fortress, 1969).

Crawley, *Dress, Drinks, Drums*
> Crawley, Ernest, *Dress, Drinks, and Drums: Further Studies of Savages and Sex* (London: Methuen, 1931).

Dautzenberg, "'Da ist nicht männlich und weiblich'"
> Dautzenberg, Gerhard, "'Da ist nicht männlich und weiblich,' Zur Interpretation von Gal 3, 28," *Kairos*, n.s. 24 (1982) 181–206.

Delling, *Paulus' Stellung*
> Delling, Gerhard, *Paulus' Stellung zu Frau und Ehe* (BWANT 56; Stuttgart: Kohlhammer, 1931).

Derrett, "Religious Hair"
> Derrett, J. Duncan M., "Religious Hair," in *Studies in the New Testament.* I: *Glimpses of the Legal and Social Presuppositions of the Authors* (Leiden: Brill, 1977) 170–73.

Dibelius, *Geisterwelt*
> Dibelius, Martin, *Die Geisterwelt in Glauben des Paulus* (Göttingen: Vandenhoeck & Ruprecht, 1909).

Donfried, *Setting*
> Donfried, Karl P., *The Setting of Second Clement in Early Christianity* (NovTSup 38; Leiden: Brill, 1974).

Evans, *Woman in the Bible*
> Evans, Mary J., *Woman in the Bible* (Exeter: Paternoster, 1983).

Feuillet, " 'Gloire de Dieu' "
> Feuillet, A., "L'homme 'gloire de Dieu' et la femme 'gloire de l'homme' (I Cor. XI.7b)," *RB* 81 (1974) 161–82.

Feuillet, "Signe de puissance"
> Feuillet, A., "Le signe de puissance sur la tête de la femme. 1 Cor. 11,10," *NRTh* 95 (1973) 945–54.

Fitzmyer, "Qumran Angelology"
> Fitzmyer, Joseph A., "A Feature of Qumran Angelology and the Angels of 1 Cor. XI.10," *NTS* 4 (1957) 48–58.

Furnish, *Moral Teaching of Paul*
> Furnish, Victor Paul, *The Moral Teaching of Paul* (Nashville: Abingdon, 1979).

Ginsburger, M., "La 'gloire' et l' 'autorité' "
> Ginsburger, M., "La 'gloire' et l' 'autorité' de la femme dans I Cor. 11,1–10," *RHPhR* 12 (1932) 245–48.

Grosheide, *Commentary*
> Grosheide, F. W., *Commentary on the First Epistle to the Corinthians* (NICNT; Grand Rapids: Eerdmans, 1953).

Héring, *First Epistle*
> Héring, Jean, *The First Epistle of St Paul to the Corinthians* (London: Epworth, 1962).

Hick, *Stellung des hl. Paulus*
> Hick, Ludwig, *Stellung des hl. Paulus zur Frau im Rahmen seiner Zeit* (Kirche und Volk 5; Köln: Amerikanisch-Ungarischer Verlag, 1957).

Hooker, "Authority"
Hooker, Morna, "Authority on Her Head: An Examination of 1 Cor. XI.10," *NTS* 10 (1964) 410–16.

Hurd, *Origin of I Corinthians*
Hurd, John C., Jr., *The Origin of I Corinthians* (London: SPCK; New York: Seabury, 1965).

Hurley, "Did Paul Require Veils"
Hurley, James B., "Did Paul Require Veils or the Silence of Women? A Consideration of I Cor 11,2–16 and I Cor 14,33b–36," *WTJ* 35 (1973) 190–220.

Hurley, *Man and Woman*
Hurley, James B., *Man and Woman in Biblical Perspective: A Study in Role Relationships and Authority* (London: Inter-Varsity, 1981).

Isaksson, *Marriage and Ministry*
Isaksson, Abel, *Marriage and Ministry in the New Temple: A Study with Special Reference to Mt. 19.3–12 and 1 Cor. 11.3–16* (Lund: Gleerup; Copenhagen: Munksgaard, 1965).

Jaubert, "Le voile"
Jaubert, Annie, "Le voile des femmes (1 Cor. XI.2–16)," *NTS* 18 (1972) 419–30.

Jervell, *Imago Dei*
Jervell, Jacob, *Imago Dei: Gen 1, 26f im Spätjudentum, in der Gnosis und in den paulinischen Briefen* (FRLANT n.s. 58; Göttingen: Vandenhoeck & Ruprecht, 1960).

Jewett, "Sexual Liberation of the Apostle Paul"
Jewett, Robert, "The Sexual Liberation of the Apostle Paul," *JAAR* 47, Supplement B (1979) 55–87.

Kähler, *Frau*
Kähler, Else, *Die Frau in den paulinischen Briefen: Unter besonderer Berücksichtigung des Begriffes der Unterordnung* (Zürich: Gotthelf–Verlag, 1960).

Kroeger, "Inquiry into Evidence of Maenadism"
Kroeger, Richard and Catherine, "An Inquiry into Evidence of Maenadism in the Corinthian Congregation," in Paul J. Achtemeier, ed., *SBL 1978 Seminar Papers* (SBLASP 14; Missoula: Scholars Press, 1978) 1. 331–38.

Leenhardt, "La place de la femme"
Leenhardt, Franz J., "La place de la femme dans l'Église d'après le Nouveau Testament," *EThR* 23 (1948) 3–50.

Leipoldt, *Die Frau*
> Leipoldt, Johannes, *Die Frau in der antiken Welt und im Urchristentum* (2d ed.; Leipzig: Koehler & Amelang, 1954).

Le origini dello gnosticismo
> Ugo Bianchi, ed., *Le origini dello gnosticismo.* Colloquio di Messina, 13–18 aprile 1966 (NumenSup 12; Leiden: Brill, 1967).

Lightfoot, *Apostolic Fathers*
> Lightfoot, J. B., *The Apostolic Fathers* (5 vols.; London and New York: Macmillan, 1885–90).

Longenecker, *New Testament Social Ethics for Today*
> Longenecker, Richard H., *New Testament Social Ethics for Today* (Grand Rapids: Eerdmans, 1984).

Meeks, "Image of the Androgyne"
> Meeks, Wayne A., "The Image of the Androgyne: Some Uses of a Symbol in Earliest Christianity," *HR* 13 (1974) 165–208.

Meier, "Veiling of Hermeneutics"
> Meier, John P. "On the Veiling of Hermeneutics (1 Cor 11:2–16)," *CBQ* 40 (1978) 212–26.

Menard, *L'Évangile selon Thomas*
> Menard, Jacques-É., *L'Évangile selon Thomas* (NHS 5; Leiden: Brill, 1975).

Merode, "Théologie primitive de la femme"
> Merode, Marie de, "Une théologie primitive de la femme?" *RThL* 9 (1978) 176–89.

Moffatt, *First Epistle*
> Moffatt, James, *The First Epistle of Paul to the Corinthians* (MNTC; New York and London: Harper, 1938).

Morris, *First Epistle*
> Morris, Leon, *The First Epistle of Paul to the Corinthians* (Tyndale New Testament Commentaries; London: Tyndale, 1958).

Murphy-O'Connor, "Sex and Logic"
> Murphy-O'Connor, Jerome, "Sex and Logic in 1 Corinthians 11:2–16," *CBQ* 42 (1980) 482–500.

Niederwimmer, *Askese und Mysterium*
> Niederwimmer, Kurt, *Askese und Mysterium: Ueber Ehe, Ehescheidung und Eheverzicht in den Anfängen des christlichen*

Glaubens (FRLANT 113; Göttingen: Vandenhoeck & Ruprecht, 1975).

Orr, *I Corinthians*
Orr, William F., and Walther, James Arthur, *I Corinthians* (AB 32; Garden City and New York: Doubleday, 1976).

Padgett, "Paul on Women in the Church"
Padgett, Alan, "Paul on Women in the Church: The Contradictions of Coiffure in 1 Corinthians 11.2–16," *JSNT* 20 (1984) 69–86.

Parvey, "Theology and Leadership"
Parvey, Constance F., "The Theology and Leadership of Women in the New Testament" in Rosemary Radford Reuther, ed., *Religion and Sexism: Images of Women in the Jewish and Christian Traditions* (New York: Simon and Schuster, 1974) 132–36.

Paulsen, "Einheit und Freiheit"
Paulsen, Henning, "Einheit und Freiheit der Söhne Gottes—Gal 3, 26–29," *ZNW* 71 (1980) 74–95.

Robertson and Plummer, *First Epistle of St Paul to the Corinthians*
Robertson, Archibald, and Plummer, Alfred, *A Critical and Exegetical Commentary on the First Epistle of St Paul to the Corinthians* (2d ed.; ICC; Edinburgh: T. & T. Clark, 1914).

Rose, "L'Épouse"
Rose, André, "L'Épouse dans l'assemblée liturgique (I Cor. 11,2–16)," *BVC* 34 (1960) 13–19.

Schmithals, *Gnosticism in Corinth*
Schmithals, Walther, *Gnosticism in Corinth* (Nashville: Abingdon, 1971).

Schüssler Fiorenza, *In Memory of Her*
Schüssler Fiorenza, Elisabeth, *In Memory of Her: A Feminist Theological Reconstruction of Christian Origins* (New York: Crossroad, 1983).

Scroggs, "Paul and the Eschatological Woman"
Scroggs, Robin, "Paul and the Eschatological Woman," *JAAR* 40 (1972) 283–303.

Senft, *La première épitre*
Senft, Christoph, *La première épitre de saint-Paul aux Corinthiens* (CNT; 2d ser. 7; Neuchâtel: Delachaux & Niestlé, 1979) 142–43.

Spicq, "Encore la 'puissance'"
> Spicq, C., "Encore la 'puissance sur la tête' (I Cor XI,10)," *RB* 48 (1939) 557–62.

Thraede, "Äger mit der Freiheit"
> Thraede, Klaus, "Äger mit der Freiheit. Die Bedeutung von Frauen in Theorie und Praxis der alten Kirche," in idem and Gerta Scharffenorth, *"Freunde in Christus werden . . ." Die Beziehung von Mann und Frau als Frage an Theologie und Kirche* (Kennzeichen 1; Gelnhausen: Burckhardthaus-Verlag; Stein: Laetare-Verlag, 1977) 31–182.

Thyen, "'. . . nicht mehr männlich und weiblich . . .'"
> Thyen, Hartwig, "'. . . nicht mehr männlich und weiblich . . .' Eine Studie zu Galater 3, 28," in idem and Frank Crusemann, eds., *Als Mann und Frau geschaffen: Exegetische Studien zur Rolle der Frau* (Kennzeichen 2; Gelnhausen: Burckhardthaus-Verlag, 1978) 107–201.

Tischleder, *Wesen und Stellung*
> Tischleder, P., *Wesen und Stellung der Frau nach der Lehre des heiligen Paulus* (Neutestamentliche Abhandlungen 10, 3–4; Münster: Aschendorff, 1923).

Van Unnik, "Les cheveux défaits"
> Van Unnik, W. C., "Les cheveux défaits des femmes baptisées. Un rite de baptême dans l'ordre ecclésiastique d'Hippolyte," *VC* 1 (1947) 77–100.

Vööbus, *Celibacy*
> Vööbus, Arthur, *Celibacy: A Requirement for Admission to Baptism in the Early Syrian Church* (Stockholm: Estonian Theological Society in Exile, 1951).

Weinel, *Paulus*
> Weinel, Heinrich, *Paulus. Der Mensch und sein Werk: Die Anfänge des Christentums, der Kirche und des Dogmas* (Lebensfragen 3; 2d ed.; Tübingen: Mohr-Siebeck, 1915).

Weiss, *Der erste Korintherbrief*
> Weiss, Johannes, *Der erste Korintherbrief* (Kritische-exegetischer Kommentar über das Neue Testament 5; 9th ed.; Göttingen: Vandenhoeck & Ruprecht, 1910).

Zscharnack, *Der Dienst der Frau*
> Zscharnack, Leopold, *Der Dienst der Frau in den ersten Jahrhunderten der christlichen Kirche* (Göttingen: Vandenhoeck & Ruprecht, 1902).

1

THERE IS NO MALE AND FEMALE

This book proposes novel interpretations of Gal 3:26-28 and 1 Cor 11:2-16, perhaps the most widely discussed passages of the New Testament for understanding early Christian male/female relations. In part, this spirited discussion issues from attempts to harmonize Paul's radical egalitarianism in Galatians with his dogmatic patriarchalism in 1 Corinthians.

Gal 3:26-28 reads:

> For in Christ Jesus you are all sons of God through faith. For as many of you as were baptized into Christ have put on Christ. There is no Jew or Greek. There is no slave or free. There is no male and female. For all of you are one in Christ Jesus.

In his popular pamphlet, *The Bible and the Role of Women: A Case Study in Hermeneutics,* Krister Stendahl speaks of the "breakthrough" of this passage insofar as it provides "glimpses which point beyond and even 'against' the prevailing view and practice of the New Testament church."[1] According to Stendahl, the grammatical shift from "There is no ... or ..." (οὐκ ἔνι ... οὐδὲ ...) to "There is no male *and* female" (οὐκ ἔνι ἄρσεν καὶ θῆλυ) is due to Paul's insistence that the division of the first humans into "male and

---

[1] Stendahl, *The Bible and the Role of Women: A Case Study in Hermeneutics* (FBBS 15; Philadelphia: Fortress, 1966) 32.

female" articulated in Gen 1:27 had been overcome in the church, the new creation. Thus, Stendahl asserts, Gal 3:28

> is directed against what we call the order of creation, and consequently it creates a tension with those biblical passages . . . by which this order of creation maintains its place in the fundamental view of the New Testament concerning the subordination of women.[2]

However, just a few years later, when scolding Corinthian women for removing their veils, Paul himself used Genesis 1–3 to establish women's ontic inferiority and social subordination:

> For a man ought not to cover his head, since he is the image and glory of God; but woman is the glory of man. For man was not made from woman, but woman from man. Neither was man created for woman, but woman for man. (1 Cor 11:7–8)

Why does Paul here seem amnesic of his daring vision of the new creation set forth in Galatians? Scholars have provided three kinds of answers:

1) Gal 3:26–28 is indeed Paul's "peak ecclesiological proposition" and a revolutionary social program, but even the apostle himself was unable to sustain its radicalism in practice.[3] Paul's bark was bolder than his bite. The champions of this interpretation are legion.[4]

---

[2] Ibid.

[3] Peter Stuhlmacher, *Der Brief an Philemon* (EKKNT; Zürich: Benziger, 1975) 67–69. Notice, however, that elsewhere he ("Christliche Verantwortung bei Paulus und seinen Schülern," *ExpTim* 28 [1968] 170–71) attributes the saying not to Paul but to the "enthusiasm" of the "Hellenistic community."

[4] E.g., Heinrich Weinel, *Paulus. Der Mensch und sein Werke: Die Anfänge des Christentums, der Kirche und des Dogmas* (Lebensfragen 3; 2d ed.; Tübingen: Mohr-Siebeck, 1915) 201; Peter Ketter, *Christus und die Frauen. Frauenleben und Frauengestalten im Neuen Testament* (Düsseldorf: Verbandsverlag weiblicher Vereine, 1933); Ludwig Hick, *Stellung des hl. Paulus zur Frau im Rahmen seiner Zeit* (Kirche und Volk 5; Köln: Amerikanisch-Ungarischer Verlag, 1957) 100–108; Else Kähler, *Die Frau in den paulinischen Briefen: Unter besonderer Berücksichtigung des Begriffes der Unterordnung* (Zürich: Gotthelf-Verlag, 1960) 198–202; and Johannes Leipoldt, *Die Frau in der antiken Welt und im Urchristentum* (3d ed.; Leipzig: Koehler and Amelang, 1965) 126. Leipoldt (pp. 126–27) compares Gal 3:28 with statements concerning the openness to women in Dionysian religion and argues that Paul was remarkably open to women's participation in the mission. This openness stands in "tension" (*Zwiespältigkeit*) with his statements concerning women's inferiority. So also Heinrich Baltensweiler, *Die Ehe im Neuen Testament. Exegetische Untersuchungen über Ehe, Ehelosigkeit und Ehescheidung*

2) Other interpreters argue that the passage presents no egalitarian social agenda at all. Paul is not calling for a new society nor demanding a collapse of hierarchical social structures; he is merely acknowledging that women and men are equal in the sight of God and have equal access to grace. [5]

(AThANT 2; Zürich: Zwingli, 1967) 264; G. B. Caird, "Paul and Women's Liberty," *BJRL* 54 (1971/72) 268–81; James E. Crouch, *The Origin and Intention of the Colossian Haustafel* (FRLANT 109; Göttingen: Vandenhoeck & Ruprecht, 1972) 144–45; Elaine H. Pagels, "Paul and Women: A Response to Recent Discussion," *JAAR* 42 (1974) 538–49; Constance F. Parvey, "The Theology and Leadership of Women in the New Testament," in Rosemary Radford Ruether, ed., *Religion and Sexism: Images of Women in the Jewish and Christian Traditions* (New York: Simon & Schuster, 1974) 132–36; Gerd Theissen, "Soteriologische Symbolik in den paulinischen Schriften," *KD* 20 (1974) 299 (see also pp. 286–87); Letty M. Russel, *Human Liberation in a Feminist Perspective—A Theology* (Philadelphia: Westminster, 1974) 33, 47; Letha Scanzoni and Nancy Hardesty, *All Were Meant To Be: A Biblical Approach to Women's Liberation* (Waco: Word Books, 1974) 15, 71–72, 204–8; Barbara Hall, "The Church in the World: Paul and Women," *TToday* 31 (1974) 51–52; Thomas R. W. Longstaff, "The Ordination of Women: A Biblical Perspective," *ATR* 57 (1975) 316–27; William O. Walker, "1 Cor 11:2–16 and Paul's Views of Women," *JBL* 94 (1975) 94–110, esp. 109–10; Patrick J. Ford, "Paul the Apostle: Male Chauvinist?" *BTB* 5 (1975) 302–11; Derwood C. Smith, "Paul and the Non-Eschatological Woman," *Ohio Journal of Religious Studies* 4 (1976) 13; Richard and Joyce Boldrey, *Chauvinist or Feminist? Paul's View of Women* (Grand Rapids: Baker Book House, 1976) 45–53; Klyne R. Snodgrass, "Paul and Women," *Covenant Quarterly* 34 (1976) 4, 12; Paul Lamarche, " 'Ni mâle, ni femelle,' Galates 3,28," *Christus* 24 (1977) 349–55; Virginia Ramey Mollenkott, *Women, Men, and the Bible* (Nashville: Abingdon, 1977) 84–85, 202–3; Peter Richardson, *Paul's Ethic of Freedom* (Philadelphia: Westminster, 1979) 75–78; Erhard S. Gerstenberger and Wolfgang Schrage, *Woman and Man* (Biblical Encounter Series; Nashville: Abingdon, 1981) 149–51; Averil Cameron, " 'Neither Male Nor Female,' " *Greece and Rome* 27 (1980) 64; and Mary J. Evans, *Women in the Bible* (Exeter: Paternoster, 1983) 62–64.

[5] Johannes Belser, "Die Frauen in den neutestamentliche Schriften," *ThQ* 90 (1909) 321–51; P. Tischleder, *Wesen und Stellung der Frau nach der Lehre des heiligen Paulus* (NTAbh 10: 3–4; Münster: Aschendorff, 1923) 108–19; Gerhard Delling, *Paulus' Stellung zu Frau und Ehe* (BWANT 56; Stuttgart: Kohlhammer, 1931) 120–21; Ernest De Witt Burton states: "That he is speaking of these distinctions from the point of view of religion is evident from the context in general . . . the passage has nothing to do with the merging of nationalities or the abolition of slavery" (*The Epistle to the Galatians* [ICC; Edinburgh: T. & T. Clark, 1921; reprinted, 1968] 206–7); and Karl Heinrich Rengstorff, "Die neutestamentlichen Mahnungen an die Frau, sich dem Manne unterzuordnen," 131–45 (esp. 140–41), in Werner Foerster, ed., *Verbum dei manet in aeternum; eine Festschrift für Prof. D. Otto Schmitz* (Witten: Luther, 1953). Rengstorff (p. 144) argues that early Christian commands that women be submissive are evidence of later reactions against those who misunderstood Gal 3:28 as a slogan for social liberation. In a later treatment, however, Rengstorff (*Mann und Frau im Urchristentum* [Arbeitsgemeinschaft für Forschung des Landes Nordrhein-Westfalen. Geisteswissenschaften 12; Köln: Westdeutscher Verlag, 1954] 7–52, esp.

3) Many others, however, argue that Gal 3:28 is not Paul's own novel creation, his peculiar "Lieblingswort,"[6] but a quotation from early Christian baptismal liturgy.[7] If so, one might account for the

---

9–22) argues that even though the intention of Gal 3:28 is primarily theological, its social implications are nevertheless radical. Others who deny Gal 3:28 its potential social radicalism are Fritz Zerbst, *The Office of Women in the Church: A Study in Practical Theology* (St. Louis: Concordia, 1955) 35; Charles C. Ryrie, *The Place of Women in the Church* (New York: Macmillan, 1958) 71; J. J. Meuzelaar, *Der Leib des Messias. Eine exegetische Studie über den Gedanken vom Leib Christi in den Paulusbriefen* (Theologische Biblioteek 35; Assen: Van Gorcum, 1961) 84–86; Albrecht Oepke, *Der Brief des Paulus an die Galater* (3d ed.; ed. Joachim Rohde; ThHKNT 9; Berlin: Evangelische Verlagsanstalt, 1973) 126; Heinrich Schlier, *Der Brief an die Galater* (MeyerK 7; Göttingen: Vandenhoeck & Ruprecht, 1962) 175; Madeleine Boucher, "Some Unexplored Parallels to 1 Cor 11:11–12 and Gal 3:28: The New Testament on the Role of Women," *CBQ* 31 (1969) 55–58; Frank Mussner, *Der Galaterbrief* (HThKNT 9; Freiburg: Herder, 1974) 264; John Jefferson Davis, "Some Reflections on Galatians 3:28, Sexual Roles, and Biblical Hermeneutics," *JETS* 19 (1976) 201–8; Robert Banks, "Paul and Women's Liberation," *Interchange* 18 (1976) 82–83; George W. Knight, "Male and Female Related He Them," *Christianity Today* April 19 (1976) 13–17; Klaus Thraede, "Ärger mit der Freiheit. Die Bedeutung von Frauen in Theorie und Praxis der alten Kirche," in Gerta Scharffenorth and idem, eds., *"Freunde in Christus werden . . ." Die Beziehung von Mann und Frau als Frage an Theologie und Kirche* (Kennzeichen 1; Gelnhausen: Burckhardthaus-Verlag; Stein: Laetare-Verlag, 1977) 102–3; Grant R. Osborne, "Hermeneutics and Women in the Church," *JETS* 20 (1977) 348–49; Susan T. Foh, *Women and the Word of God: A Response to Biblical Feminism* (Philadelphia: Presbyterian and Reformed Publishing Co., 1979) 140–43; Stephen B. Clark, *Man and Woman in Christ: An Examination of the Roles of Men and Women in Light of Scripture and the Social Sciences* (Ann Arbor: Servant Books, 1980) 137–63; and James B. Hurley, *Man and Woman in Biblical Perspective: A Study in Role Relationships and Authority* (London: Inter-Varsity, 1981) 125–28.

[6] The expression is that of Hans Lietzmann, *Die Briefe des Apostels Paulus*, vol. 1: *Die vier Hauptbriefe* (Tübingen: Mohr-Siebeck, 1910) 245.

[7] Franz Leenhardt, "La place de la femme dans l'église d'après le Nouveau Testament," *ÉThR* 23 (1948) 31; Jacob Jervell, *Imago Dei: Gen 1, 26f im Spätjudentum, in der Gnosis und in den paulinischen Briefen* (FRLANT 76, n.s. 58; Göttingen: Vandenhoeck & Ruprecht, 1960) 294–95; Georg Günther Blum, "Das Amt der Frau im Neuen Testament," *NovT* 7 (1964) 155–56; Ernst Käsemann, *Jesus Means Freedom* (3d ed.; Philadelphia: Fortress, 1969) 64–65; Robin Scroggs, "Paul and the Eschatological Woman," *JAAR* 40 (1972) 291–93; Walther Schmithals, *Gnosticism in Corinth* (Nashville: Abingdon, 1971) 239, n. 162; Siegfried Schulz, "Evangelium und Welt. Hauptprobleme einer Ethik des Neuen Testaments," in Hans Dieter Betz and Luise Schottroff, eds., *Neues Testament und christliche Existenz* (Festschrift for Herbert Braun; Tübingen: Mohr-Siebeck, 1973) 491; Hans Dieter Betz, "Geist, Freiheit und Gesetz: Die Botschaft des Paulus an die Gemeinden in Galatien," *ZThK* 71 (1974) 81 (This article has been translated into English: "Spirit, Freedom, and Law: Paul's Message to the Galatian Churches," *Svensk exegetisk årsbok* 39 (1974) 145–60.); and idem, *Galatians: A Commentary on Paul's Letter to the Churches in Galatia* (Hermeneia; Philadel-

friction between Galatians 3 and 1 Corinthians 11 as evidence of incongruity between a liberating pre-Pauline movement and Paul himself. Inasmuch as the solution proposed in this study falls generally under this category, it will prove helpful to examine in some detail how various scholars have attempted to isolate the traditional saying and to relocate it in its more native theological environment.

1.1 Galatians 3:26–28 as Pre-Pauline Tradition

Interpreters largely agree about what is tradition and what redaction in Gal 3:26–28. One might delineate this consensus as follows:

1) Gal 3:26–28, 1 Cor 12:13, and Col 3:9–11 all hark back to a traditional baptismal saying:[8]

---

phia: Fortress, 1979) 181; Wayne A. Meeks, "The Image of the Androgyne: Some Uses of a Symbol in Earliest Christianity," *HR* 13 (1974) 165–208; Kurt Niederwimmer, *Askese und Mysterium: Über Ehe, Ehescheidung und Eheverzicht in den Anfängen des christlichen Glaubens* (FRLANT 113; Göttingen: Vandenhoeck & Ruprecht, 1975) 178; Dieter Lührmann, "Wo man nicht mehr Sklave oder Freier ist. Überlegungen zur Struktur frühchristlicher Gemeinden," *Wort und Dienst* n.s. 13 (1975) 57–58; Michel Bouttier, "*Complexio Oppositorum*: sur les formules de I Cor. XII. 13; Gal. III. 26–28; Col. III. 10, 11," *NTS* 23 (1976) 1–19; Howard Loewen, "The Pauline View of Women," *Direction* 6 (1977) 3–20; Marie de Merode, "Une théologie primitive de la femme?" *RThL* 9 (1978) 176–89, esp. 180; Hartwig Thyen, "'... nicht mehr männlich und weiblich ...' Eine Studie zu Galater 3, 28," in Frank Crüsemann and Hartwig Thyen, eds., *Als Mann und Frau geschaffen: Exegetische Studien zur Rolle der Frau* (Kennzeichen 2; Gelnhausen: Burckhardthaus-Verlag; Stein: Laetare-Verlag, 1978) 107–201, esp. 138–39; Victor Paul Furnish, *The Moral Teaching of Paul* (Nashville: Abingdon, 1979) 93; Henning Paulsen, "Einheit und Freiheit der Söhne Gottes—Gal 3, 26–29," *ZNW* 71 (1980) 77–78; Bernard H. Brinsmead, *Galatians— Dialogical Response to Opponents* (SBLDS 65; Scholars, 1982) 146–50, 157–58; J. Louis Martyn, "Galatians 3:28, Faculty Appointments and the Overcoming of Christological Amnesia," *Katallagete* 8 (1982) 39–44; Elisabeth Schüssler Fiorenza, *In Memory of Her: A Feminist Theological Reconstruction of Christian Origins* (New York: Crossroads, 1983) 205–41; and Richard N. Longenecker, *New Testament Social Ethics for Today* (Grand Rapids: Eerdmans, 1984) 31–34.

[8] Gerhard Dautzenberg disagrees ("'Da ist nicht männlich und weiblich,' Zur Interpretation von Gal 3, 28," *Kairos* n.s. 24 (1982) 181–206). In his judgment (pp. 200–202), the tradition behind the text is simply the actual overcoming of sociological differences in Pauline communities. Francesco Saracino ("Forma e funzione di una formula paolina: Gal. 3, 28," *RevistB* 28 [1980] 345–406) also denies these texts relate to a pre-Pauline formula. Saracino contends that Paul, by listing polar opposites, employed a common literary device, not a traditional formula. Gal 3:28 is Paul's own crafted formulation serving to cap off his discussion of the Law.

Gal 3:27–28	1 Cor 12:13	Col 3:10–11
For in Christ Jesus all of you are sons of God through faith, for		
	For also in one spirit	
as many of you as were baptized into Christ	all of us were baptized into one body,	
(εἰς Χριστὸν ἐβαπτίσθητε)	(εἰς ἓν σῶμα ἐβαπτίσθημεν	Putting off the old human with its deeds, and
have put on Christ.		putting on the new
(Χριστὸν ἐνεδύσασθε)		(ἐνδυσάμενοι
	renewed unto knowledge according to the image of the one who created it,	τὸν νέον)
There is no Jew or Greek.	whether Jews or Greeks,	where there is no Greek and Jew,
(οὐκ ἔνι Ἰουδαῖος οὐδὲ Ἕλλην)	(εἴτε Ἰουδαῖοι εἴτε Ἕλληνες)	(ὅπου οὐκ ἔνι Ἕλλην καὶ Ἰουδαῖος) circumcision and uncircumcision, barbarian, Scythian,
There is no slave or free.	whether slaves or free.	slave, free.
(οὐκ ἔνι δοῦλος οὐδὲ ἐλεύθερος) There is no male and female.	(εἴτε δοῦλοι εἴτε ἐλεύθεροι)	(δοῦλος, ἐλεύθερος)
For all (πάντες) of you are one (εἷς) in Christ Jesus.	And all (πάντες) have drunk of one spirit (ἓν πνεῦμα)	But Christ is all things (πάντα) and in all things (πᾶσιν).

Wayne Meeks lists the following features to illustrate what he calls a "consistency of major motifs": baptism into Christ, garment imagery, pairs of opposites, and concluding statement of unity.[9]

---

[9] Meeks, "Image of the Androgyne," 180–83.

2) Of the three versions, that in Galatians is the most original:

a) Gal 3:26–28 stands in a mediating position between the other two.[10]

b) Colossians was not written by Paul and may in fact be directly dependent on Galatians.[11]

c) Gal 3:26–28 stands out from its context more clearly than 1 Cor 12:13 and Col 3:10–11, both grammatically (the second person plural, whereas the context is third plural) and thematically (only the pair Jew/Greek is directly germane to the argument and the introduction of baptism into the discussion seems quite unnecessary[12]).

d) The pair male/female is less likely to have been added by Paul than to have fallen out in 1 Corinthians and Colossians.

3) Even though Gal 3:26–28 refers to tradition, it clearly has been reworked by Paul for use in Galatians. In order better to isolate these redactional alterations, scholars generally break the text down into the following sense lines:

(26) a For you all are sons of God in Christ Jesus through faith.
(27) b For as many of you as have been baptized into Christ
      c have put on Christ.
(28) d There is no Jew or Greek.
      e There is no slave or free.
      f There is no male and female.
      g For you all are one in Christ Jesus.

4) Pauline redaction includes:

a) All of lines "a" and "g."
   i) Both lines are grammatically identical to 1 Thess 5:5,

---

[10] Bouttier, "*Complexio Oppositorum*," 11.

[11] For evidence of this dependence see the discussion of Eduard Lohse, *Colossians and Philemon* (Hermeneia; Philadelphia: Fortress, 1971) 182.

[12] Baptism interrupts the flow of the argument, even though the interruption does not involve a substantive theological contradiction. See Hermann-Josef Venetz, "'Christus anziehen,' Eine Exegese zu Gal. 3.26–28 als Beitrag zum paulinischen Taufverständis," *Freiburger Zeitschrift für Philosophie und Theologie* 20 (1973) 3–36; and S. Légasse, "Foi et baptême chez saint Paul: Étude de Galates 3,26–27," *BLE* 74 (1973) 81–102.

apparently Paul's own formulation: "For you are all sons of light."

ii) These two lines do not form a traditional *inclusio* but conform to a literary device used elsewhere for quoting tradition without unduly breaking the flow of the larger context by repeating at the end of the saying the last phrase before the saying.

iii) Both lines are packed with distinctively Pauline expressions. The phrase "through faith" (διὰ τῆς πίστεως) not only breaks the parallelism with line "g" but is found frequently in Paul.[13] The words "in Christ Jesus" (ἐν Χριστῷ Ἰησοῦ) in lines "a" and "g" also are characteristically Pauline.[14] Paul calls believers "sons" (υἱοί, line "a") also in Rom 8:14, 19; 9:26; Gal 3:7; 4:6, 7; and 1 Thess 5:5.

iv) Line "a" is directly related to the preceding context, as the word "for" makes clear, and line "g" is grammatically and thematically linked with what immediately follows: "And if you are Christ's. . . ."

b) All of line "b" may be redaction as well. To baptize "into Christ" is an expression unique to Paul in the New Testament. The reference to baptism probably is not part of the saying itself but an indication of its ritual context.

5) The traditional features of the saying include:

a) the reference to baptism as an indication of the *Sitz im Leben*;

b) the garment imagery in line "c," which refers to the exchange of garments in baptism;

c) the second person plural ("you"), inasmuch as the preceding context is in the third plural;

d) the pairs of opposites in lines "d," "e," and "f," especially the last pair; (When Paul speaks of men and women elsewhere he uses "male/female" [ἄρσεν/θῆλυ] only in Rom 1:27 when sexual activity is explicitly meant. When he speaks of the

---

[13] Rom 1:12; 8:22, 25, 27, 30, 31; 4:13; 2 Cor 5:7; Gal 2:16; 3:14, 26; Phil 3:9; 1 Thess 1:7; see also the uses of ἐκ τῆς πίστεως which are even more numerous.

[14] Rom 3:24; 8:1, 2, 39; 15:17; 16:3; 1 Cor 1:2, 4, 30; 4:15, 17; 15:31; 16:24; Gal 2:4; 5:6; Phil 1:1, 26; 2:5; 3:14; 4:7, 19, 21; 1 Thess 2:14; 5:18; Phlm 23; "in Christ": Rom 9:1; 12:5; 16:7, 9, 10; 1 Cor 3:1; 4:10, 15; 15:18, 19, 22; 2 Cor 2:14, 17; 3:14; 5:17, 19; 12:2, 19; Gal 1:22; 2:17; Phil 1:13; 2:1; 1 Thess 4:16; Phlm 8, 20; and "in Jesus Christ": Gal 3:14; 1 Thess 1:1.

relationship of the sexes otherwise he uses "man/woman" [ἀνήρ/γυνή].[15])

e) probably the chiasm that alternates the order of privilege and subordination in the pairs: ab/ba/ab; (Parallelism would require Jew/Greek, *free/slave*, male/female.)

f) the allusion is to Genesis, indicated by the apparent influence of Gen 1:27 (LXX) on "male *and* female," breaking the pattern of "There is no . . . *or*. . . ."

When alchemized in this manner by form-critics, Gal 3:26–28 yields the following traditional deposit:

> . . . you have put on Christ.
> There is no Jew or Greek.
> There is no slave or free.
> There is no male and female.

Once such an utterance precipitates out of its literary setting, one may speculate on its preliterary origin, including its most likely performative setting or *Sitz im Leben*. Presumably the performative setting is baptism, but scholars part ways in locating the saying in one of the many subclassifications of primitive Christianity. One can group these rival proposals into three categories: (1) Paul's own circle; (2) Pauline communities; or (3) parties opposed to Paul.

Paul's Own Circle

Robin Scroggs argues that the tradition coincides with "the roots of his [i.e., Paul's] understanding of the Gospel,"[16] and is "an essential corollary to his deepest theological conviction."[17] Likewise, Michel Bouttier claims that the formula arose in Pauline circles and is consistent with his understanding of the transforming power of the gospel, even though in certain situations, because complete social integration is unattainable prior to the parousia, Paul had to compromise its overly enthusiastic social agenda.[18] This essentially is

---

[15] Rom 7:2–3; 1 Cor 7:2–4, 10–11, 13–16, 39; 11:3–14.

[16] Scroggs, "Paul and the Eschatological Woman," 293.

[17] Ibid., 288.

[18] Bouttier, "*Complexio Oppositorum*," 10, 15–18.

the understanding also of Ernst Käsemann,[19] Dieter Lührmann,[20] and Henning Paulsen.[21]

According to Hans Dieter Betz, Gal 3:26-28 with its "three political-social, programmatic slogans,"[22] is a baptismal beatitude reflecting the revolutionary changes caused by Paul's original preaching in Galatia. The theme of "freedom" so pervasive in Galatians is not just freedom from law; it is indissolubly bound to the social emancipation that characterized the Galatians' first responses to the gospel.[23] By heeding recently arrived "Judaizers," they had compromised this freedom in the name of holiness and Torah obedience. Therefore, Paul quotes the baptismal formula to remind them of the radical egalitarianism expressed in their common rite of initiation. Paul still fully endorses this utopian ideal in Galatians, but by the time he wrote 1 Corinthians, perhaps because of overenthusiasm at Corinth, he changed his mind about the unity of men and women—whence the absence of the male/female pair in 1 Cor 12:13.[24]

Pauline Communities apart from Paul

Franz Leenhardt thought Gal 3:28 came not from Paul's inner circle but originally was a slogan Galatian women used to justify their equality with men in their newfound freedom.[25] Siegfried Schulz argues that Gal 3:27-28 and parallels reflect an "enthusiastic-dualistic battlecry,"[26] such as may have been used among the "spiritual" at Corinth. Their baptism into the heavenly Christ and consequent alienation from the world resulted in emancipation from

[19] *Jesus Means Freedom* (3d ed.; Philadelphia: Fortress, 1969) 64-65.

[20] "Wo man nicht mehr Sklave oder Freier ist," 55-71.

[21] "Einheit und Freiheit," 94-95. Paulsen argues that Gal 3:26-29 reflects the actual historical experience of social equality in Pauline churches. Paul theologizes from this experience in Galatians to make a particular point concerning Jews and Greeks but does not advance the formula as a "social program" (p. 94).

[22] Betz, "Geist, Freiheit und Gesetz: Die Botschaft des Paulus an die Gemeinden in Galatien," *ZThK* 71 (1974) 83 (This article has been translated into English: "Spirit, Freedom, and Law: Paul's Message to the Galatian Churches," *Svensk exegetisk årsbok* 39 (1974) 145-60.).

[23] Ibid., 84-85.

[24] Betz, *Galatians*, 200.

[25] Leenhardt, "La place de la femme," 31.

[26] Schulz, "Evangelium und Welt. Hauptprobleme einer Ethik des Neuen Testaments," in Hans Dieter Betz and Luise Schottroff, eds., *Neues Testament und christliche Existenz* (Festschrift for Herbert Braun; Tübingen: Mohr-Siebeck, 1973) 491-92.

religious, social, and even sexual distinctions. This was never Paul's own position.

Meeks too claims that Paul, in spite of his employment of the formula in Galatians and 1 Corinthians, found himself uneasy and even at odds with the tradition, especially with its attending midrashic "myth." Gal 3:28 belongs to baptismal ritual which symbolized the initiate's return to the androgyny of the first human. Jews, Christians, and Gnostics often assumed Adam originally was masculofeminine. "Putting off the old human" in Colossians refers to the removal of the "robes of skin" in Gen 3:21, often believed to be the body. One must be reclothed in the image of God; that is, one must "put on Christ" or "the new human." Meeks further demonstrates that one finds this anthropological imagery and *Urzeit-Endzeit* sacramentalism most frequently in Christian Gnosticism and that it exerted its influence already in Pauline circles, most notably at Corinth. Thus Meeks concludes:

> The differentiation of male and female could therefore become an important symbol for the fundamental order of the world, while any modification of the role differences could become a potent symbol of social criticism or even of total rejection of the existing order. When early Christians in the area of the Pauline mission adapted the Adam-Androgyne myth to the eschatological sacrament of baptism, they thus produced a powerful and prolific set of images. If in baptism the Christian has put on again the image of the Creator, in whom "there is no male and female," then for him the old world has passed away and, behold! the new has come. [27]

This sacramental "realized eschatology" characterized the Corinthian "spiritual," whose "appropriation of the reunification symbols" Paul viewed as "an implicit rejection of the *created* order." [28] Paul agreed with the "spirituals" with respect to the desirability of a reunification of the sexes and a return to the divine image, but he protested that this reunification was unattainable prior to the eschaton.

> Therefore Paul accepts and even insists upon the equality of role of man and woman in this community which is formed already by the Spirit that belongs to the end of days. The new order, the order of man in the image of God, was already taking form

---

[27] Meeks, "Image of the Androgyne," 207.
[28] Ibid., 208; the emphasis is Meeks'.

in the patterns of leadership of the new community. Yet the old order was to be allowed still its symbolic claims, for the Christian lived yet in the world, in the "land of unlikeness," until the time should come for the son himself to submit to the Father, that God might be all in all.[29]

The brief precis offered here does little justice to this remarkably far-reaching and seminal essay. The most perspicacious interpreters of Gal 3:27–28 since Meeks are all his debtors.[30] The present study too, in spite of its serious disagreements, has been nourished throughout by foraging in the luxuriant footnotes of "The Image of the Androgyne."

Elisabeth Schüssler Fiorenza too sees Gal 3:26–28 as a pre-Pauline "baptismal confession,"[31] which expresses "the theological self-understanding of the Christian missionary movement."[32] The theological conviction lying behind "There is no male and female" is not the androgyne myth but the insistence that "patriarchal marriage—and sexual relations between male and female—is no longer constitutive of the new community in Christ."[33]

> While the baptismal declaration in Gal 3:28 offered a new religious vision to women and slaves, it denied all male religious prerogatives in the Christian communtiy based on gender roles. Just as born Jews had to abandon the privileged notion that they alone were the chosen people of God, so masters had to relinquish their power over slaves, and husbands that over wives and children. . . . The legal-societal and cultural-religious male privileges were no longer valid for Christians. Insofar as this egalitarian Christian self-understanding did away with all male privileges of religion, class, and caste, it allowed not only gentiles and slaves but also women to exercise leadership functions within the missionary movement.[34]

According to Schüssler Fiorenza, the significance of the saying for shaping early Christian social life is apparent in Paul's struggle to

---

[29] Ibid.

[30] E.g., Hartwig Thyen ("'. . . nicht mehr männlich und weiblich . . .'") adopts Meeks' proposal. See also Robert Jewett, "The Sexual Liberation of the Apostle Paul," *JAAR* 47 Supplement B (1979) 64–65.

[31] Schüssler Fiorenza, *In Memory of Her*, 208.

[32] Ibid., 199.

[33] Ibid., 211.

[34] Ibid., 217–18.

modify the saying and to correct some of its more deleterious results in 1 Corinthians 7 and 11–14. Although Paul did not violate Gal 3:28 in principle, his modifications restricted

> more severely the active participation of Christian wives in the worship of the community. His use of the virgin-bride metaphor for the church, as well as his figurative characterization of his apostleship as fatherhood, opens the door for a reintroduction of patriarchal values and sexual dualities.[35]

In Schüssler Fiorenza's hands Gal 3:28 functions as a ruler for measuring the social liberation of early Christian authors—including Paul himself. I trust it will be clear that my disagreement with her on the meaning and origin of Gal 3:28 in no way diminishes my admiration for *In Memory of Her*, a landmark in the study of women in the early church and a monument to contemporary feminist biblical scholarship.

Circles Opposed to Paul

Other scholars remove Paul even further from the origin of the baptismal saying. According to Georg Günther Blum, Paul here appropriates this "gnostische Terminologie" of a sacramental unification of the sexes but could never have consented to its challenge of the subordination of women implied in the order of creation.[36] The passage is more Gnostic than Pauline. Walther Schmithals claims the saying is "pure gnosticism."[37]

Bernard H. Brinsmead agrees with Meeks that the androgyne myth lies behind Gal 3:26–28, but he insists that Paul was the first to apply the traditional saying to baptism. Originally it referred to circumcision and was current among nomistic Jewish-Christians, such as the Judaizers in Galatia.[38] To make his case, Brinsmead argues that baptism, though explicitly mentioned only here, is central to Paul's polemics throughout Galatians. There is, however, a fatal flaw in his argument. It is difficult to imagine how the removal of penis foreskin could have symbolized "There is no male and female." Castration perhaps; circumcision never. Surely baptism—

---

[35] Ibid., 235–36.
[36] Blum, "Das Amt der Frau im Neuen Testament," *NovT* 7 (1964) 155–56.
[37] Schmithals, *Gnosticism in Corinth*, 239.
[38] Brinsmead, *Galatians—Dialogical Response to Opponents*, 139–61.

applicable to both sexes and requiring no particular anatomical equipment—provides the more likely original setting.[39]

From this survey it is apparent that Gal 3:28 stands at the center of a debate over the role of women in early Christianity. Most interpreters agree that the passage celebrates the abolition of social distinctions in the Christian community, but they disagree wildly in locating the origin of the passage. Is it Paul's own formulation or is it traditional? If traditional, did it originate within Paul's own circles, in the Gentile mission apart from Paul, or even in circles rival to Paul? Did Paul agree with it enthusiastically when writing the Galatians and later change his mind, or did he use it with mental reservations already in Galatians? Who was more committed to sexual equality: Paul or the pre-Pauline bearers of the tradition? If Gal 3:26–28 is indeed a window through which one can see pre-Pauline tradition at work, precisely what does one see?

1.2 Galatians 3:26–28 and a Dominical Saying

This study attempts to provide an original solution to these questions by suggesting that the traditional features of Gal 3:28 are due to Paul's dependence on a saying found in the *Gospel of the Egyptians, 2 Clement,* and the *Gospel of Thomas.* For ease of reference, I shall refer to this tradition as the Dominical Saying inasmuch as it is ascribed to Jesus in each of its citations. By calling the saying "dominical" I am making no judgment explicit or implicit concerning its authenticity as a saying of Jesus. Compare the following passage with Gal 3:27–28:

Dominical Saying	*Gal 3:27–28*
	For as many of you as have been baptized into Christ have
When you tread upon the garment ($\check{\epsilon}\nu\delta\upsilon\mu\alpha$) of shame, and when the two become one,	put on ($\dot{\epsilon}\nu\epsilon\delta\acute{\upsilon}\sigma\alpha\sigma\theta\epsilon$) Christ. There is no Jew or Greek. There is no slave or free.
and the male with the female neither male nor female ($o\check{\upsilon}\tau\epsilon$ $\check{\alpha}\rho\rho\epsilon\nu$ $o\check{\upsilon}\tau\epsilon$ $\theta\hat{\eta}\lambda\upsilon$).[40]	There is no male and female ($o\grave{\upsilon}\kappa$ $\check{\epsilon}\nu\iota$ $\check{\alpha}\rho\sigma\epsilon\nu$ $\kappa\alpha\grave{\iota}$ $\theta\hat{\eta}\lambda\upsilon$). For you all are one in Christ Jesus.

[39] Some cultures circumcize women as well as men, but I know of no evidence of female circumcision in circles even remotely related to Paul.

[40] Clem. Al. *Strom.* 3.13.92, quoting the *Gospel of the Egyptians.*

The similarities are substantial. Furthermore, it is precisely those features of Gal 3:27–28 widely considered traditional that we find here as well. Both begin with garment images using cognate words (ἔνδυμα, ἐνδύω); both begin in the second person plural ("you"); both speak of unification ("the two are one"; "you all are one"); both list pairs of opposites; and in both the final pairing is male/female (οὔτε ἄρρεν οὔτε θῆλυ; οὐκ ἔνι ἄρσεν καὶ θῆλυ). Surely there is some genetic relationship between them.

Those recognizing these similarities unanimously have judged the version in Galatians the more original, presumably because Galatians was written decades before the *Gospel of the Egyptians*, *2 Clement*, and the *Gospel of Thomas*.[41] But one must be cautious in trusting the relative dates of documents when monitoring the development of oral traditions. In this case, the earliest document contains the most derivative version.

This book will argue that the Dominical Saying was known and used by Paul, *mutatis mutandis*, in Gal 3:26–28. From its philosophical seeds in hellenized Judaism, a saying sprouted in the soil of Gentile Christianity which Paul tried to nip in the bud, but which nonetheless blossomed in second- and third-century Gnosticism. Furthermore, I shall argue that both Paul and the primary transmitters of the saying were committed to sexual equality but in radically different and theologically incompatible ways. Sexual equality as expressed in the Dominical Saying resulted from a return to primordial androgyny in a baptism regarded as putting off the body. In its denial of sexual differentiation the saying spoke of the individual soul's achievement of the divine image, immaterial and sexually unified. Paul, however, subtly altered the wording of the saying and profoundly altered its ethical consequences. As it now stands, the denial of social divisions in Gal 3:28 is the apostle's own original declaration and not an echo of a more socially egalitarian tradition still audible in spite of Paul's attempts to muffle it.

---

[41] Meeks, "Image of the Androgyne," 193–97; Betz, *Galatians*, 195–96; Paulsen, "Einheit und Freiheit," 80–84; Kurt Niederwimmer, *Askese und Mysterium*, 177–78; Marie de Merode, "Une théologie de la femme?," 188; Hartwig Thyen, "'. . . nicht mehr männlich und weiblich . . . ,'" 140–41; Gerhard Dautzenberg, "'Da ist nicht männlich und weiblich,'" 189–93; Brinsmead, *Galatians—Dialogical Response to Opponents*, 150–51—he claims both sayings go back to a common tradition but he still seems to give temporal priority to the version in Galatians; and Schüssler Fiorenza, *In Memory of Her*, 211–13.

Of course, this still leaves us with the difficulty of harmonizing Gal 3:26–28 with Paul's reaffirmation of sexual distinctions and male superiority in 1 Cor 11:2–16. I shall contend that this text too must be read in light of the baptismal anthropology presupposed by the Dominical Saying, and when so read the incongruities largely disappear.

In order to show this, Chapter 2 articulates the meaning of the Dominical Saying, its ritual performative setting, its philosophical roots, and its currency among Christian Gnostics. Chapter 3 shows how Paul himself opposed this theology and sacramentology when writing 1 Corinthians. Chapter 4 discusses how Paul's arguments with the Corinthians conform to his alteration of the saying in Galatians 3. It should then be apparent that the prevailing view championed by Meeks and Schüssler Fiorenza is wrong. Gal 3:27–28 is not a verbal window through which one sees the sexual egalitarianism of pre-Pauline tradition. Instead, it is a verbal prism refracting the theology of Paul's opponents into an original reformulation. "There is no male and female" is Paul's vision of sexual equality in his communities as they *should* be, not a witness to conditions in these communities as they were in fact.

2

THE FORM AND MEANING OF
THE DOMINICAL SAYING

The Dominical Saying appears three times in early Christian literature and in three quite different forms. In 1912, before the
discovery of the Coptic *Gospel of Thomas*, Kirsopp Lake recognized
the similarities between the sayings in the *Gospel of the Egyptians*, *2
Clement*, and Oxyrhynchus Papyrus 655—now recognized to have
been a Greek fragment of the *Gospel of Thomas*—and he observed,
"The problem of the mutual relations between these documents is
still unsolved."[1] It remains unsolved, and now the problem is more
complex than anyone in 1912 could have expected. The 1946
discovery of the Coptic *Gospel of Thomas* in the Nag Hammadi cache
has unearthed another parallel to this saying entirely unknown to
Lake. It appears in a logion generally regarded as "one of the most
complicated passages in the *Gospel of Thomas*."[2] Therefore, the task
of describing the relations between these texts is as formidable as it
is overdue. In this Chapter we shall examine the form of the saying,
its most plausible and original meaning, and its performative setting.

---

[1] *The Apostolic Fathers* (ed. and trans. Kirsopp Lake; 2 vols.; New York: G. P.
Putnam's Sons, 1912–13) 2. 147 n. 1.

[2] Bertil Gärtner, *The Theology of the Gospel According to Thomas* (New York:
Harper, 1961) 218. This judgment is shared by Karl H. Rengstorff, "Urchristliches
Kerygma und 'gnostische' Interpretation in einigen Sprüchen des Thomasevangeli-
ums," in Ugo Bianchi, ed., *Le origini dello gnosticismo*. Colloquio di Messina, 13–18
aprile 1966. (NumenSup 12; Leiden: Brill, 1967) 565.

2.1 The Form of the Saying

The *Gospel of the Egyptians* (not to be confused with its namesake from Nag Hammadi) probably was written sometime during the first half of the second century and was popular in Egypt already by 200 CE.[3] Of this gospel only a few fragments remain—all of them in the writings of Clement of Alexandria.[4] According to Clement, the gospel included this:

> When Salome asked when the events about which she inquired would be known, the Lord said: "When you tread upon the garment of shame, and when the two are one, and the male with the female neither male nor female."[5]

The document called *2 Clement* is an anonymous sermon from the beginning of the second century or the end of the first.[6] Although the identity of the preacher is unknown, its place of origin probably was Corinth.[7] If this date and location are correct, a saying almost identical to that in the *Gospel of the Egyptians* was quoted in a Corinthian sermon early in the second century.

> For the Lord himself, when asked by someone when his Kingdom will come, said: "When the two are one, and the outside as the inside, and the male with the female neither male nor female. When you have done these things the Kingdom of my Father will come." (*2 Clement* 12.2)

---

[3] The Valentinian Theodotus (160–70) and the Docetist Julius Cassianus quote it as an authority, and it was used by Naassenes and Sabellians long after Origen said it was rejected by dominant Alexandrian Christianity.

[4] Origen (*First Homily on Luke 1:1*), Hippolytus (*Haer.* 5.7), and Epiphanius (*Pan.* 50.12.2) all mention a *Gospel of the Egyptians* but add nothing to our knowledge of its content. For an analysis of the futile attempts to attribute other materials to this gospel see that of Wilhelm Schneemelcher, *NTApoc*, 1. 166–78.

[5] Clem. Al. *Strom.* 3.13.92.

[6] J. B. Lightfoot (*The Apostolic Fathers* [5 vols.; London and New York: Macmillan, 1885–90] 1. 203–4) suggests an early second-century date; and Karl P. Donfried (*The Setting of Second Clement in Early Christianity* [NovTSup 38; Leiden: Brill, 1974] 1–2) argues for a first-century date.

[7] The book was wrongly ascribed to Clement of Rome at a very early date, and there is no apparent reason why it would have been circulated with *1 Clement* had it not been associated with the Corinthian church. See also Lightfoot, *Apostolic Fathers*, 1. 197; and Donfried, *Setting*, 2–7.

Though scholars still dispute the date of the Nag Hammadi *Gospel of Thomas*, some of its traditions undoubtedly circulated already in the first century.[8] In logion 37 and in Oxyrhynchus 655, probably a Greek version of that logion, we again find reference to treading on a garment.[9]

> His disciples said, "When will you appear to us, and when will we see you?" Jesus said, "When you take off your shame (ⲍⲟⲧⲁⲛ ⲉⲧⲉⲧⲛ̄ϣⲁⲕⲉⲕ ⲧⲏⲩⲧⲛ̄ ⲉⲍⲏⲩ ⲙⲡⲉⲧⲛ̄ϣⲓⲡⲉ), and take your garments and put them under your feet, like these little children and tread on them, then [you will see] the Son of the Living (One) and you shall not fear." (*Gos. Thom.* 37)[10]

> His disciples say to him, "When will you appear to us, and when will we see you?" He says, "When you take off your garments and are not ashamed [lacuna]." (Ox. Pap. 655)

The primary difference between these two versions is the simile of the little children in *Gos. Thom.* 37, which also appears in 21a as an allegory:

> Mary said to Jesus, "Who are your disciples like?" He said, "They are like little children who dwell in a field not theirs. When the masters of the field come they will say, 'Give our field to us.' They take off their garments before them to release it to them and to give back their field to them." (*Gos. Thom.* 21a)

---

[8] E.g., Gilles Quispel ("Gnosticism and the New Testament," in James Philip Hyatt, ed., *The Bible in Modern Scholarship* [Nashville: Abingdon, 1965] 253) dates it to about 140, as does Henri-Charles Puech (*NTApoc*, 1. 305). Helmut Koester (*Introduction to the New Testament*. [2 vols.; Foundations and Facets; Philadelphia: Fortress, 1982; Berlin/New York: DeGruyter, 1983] 2. 152) dates it to the first century.

[9] Joseph A. Fitzmyer, "The Oxyrhynchus *Logoi* and the Coptic Gospel According to Thomas," *TS* 20 (1959) 551–56. This article also appears in idem, *Essays on the Semitic Background of the New Testament* (London: Chapman, 1971; Sources for Biblical Study 5; Missoula: Scholars, 1974). I have intentionally not followed the brilliant but highly conjectural reconstructions of the end of the text by Fitzmyer (pp. 543–46) and by Robert A. Kraft, "Oxyrhynchus Papyrus 655 Reconsidered," *HTR* 54 (1961) 253–62.

[10] This translation needs defending at one point. Influenced by Ox. Pap. 655, the Brill translation and most scholars have taken ⲙⲡⲉⲧⲛ̄ϣⲓⲡⲉ as the negative first perfect of ϣⲓⲡⲉ and read "are not ashamed." It is quite unlikely, however, that anyone would have translated the Coptic this way had Ox. Pap. 655 not been available. ⲙⲡⲉⲧⲛ̄ϣⲓⲡⲉ is more likely the object of ⲉⲧⲉⲧⲛ̄ϣⲁⲕⲉⲕ ⲉⲍⲏⲩ. If so, it would appear likely that the Coptic *Gospel of Thomas* translated a Greek text unlike Ox. Pap. 655 and closer to the reading in the *Gospel of the Egyptians*.

Of course, these references to "garments of shame" by themselves fail to demonstrate the presence of the Dominical Saying. However, just a few lines after this allegory of the children's garments Jesus tells his disciples the two must become one:

> Jesus said to them: "When you make the two one, and you make the inside as the outside, and the outside as the inside, and the above as the below, and when you make the male with the female into a single one, so that the male will not be male and the female not be female. When you make eyes in the place of an eye, and a hand in the place of a hand, and a foot in the place of a foot—an image in the place of an image—then you shall enter the Kingdom." (*Gos. Thom.* 22b)

Inasmuch as one can attribute to redaction the intervening lines between 21a (the allegory of the children removing clothes) and 22b (the two becoming one),[11] it would appear that the tradition behind

---

[11] If the evangelist did indeed know of the saying in a form similar to that in the *Gospel of the Egyptians*, one must account for the following as redaction: (1) "When you tread upon the garment of shame" in the form of a story (*Gos. Thom.* 21a, paralleled in 37); (2) the story of the householder and the thief (21b); (3) the plea for a wise interpreter (21c); and (4) the introduction to the saying in logion 22 (22a).

The explanation of the first addition depends on the answer to the second: why might the evangelist have inserted the story of the householder and thief (21b; compare this with the similar story in Q [Matt 24:43–44 // Luke 12:39–40])? By introducing the story with διὰ τοῦτο, the author linked it to the story concerning the little children in the field. Translated into structural units the two look like this:

(21a)
Disciple (weak) in the enemy's realm (field)
Enemy comes to take his own
Disciples takes off clothes (nonresistance)
Gives up what is not his

(21b)
Disciple (strong) in own realm (house)
Enemy comes to take not his own
Disciple binds on clothes (resistance)
Guards what is his

Taken together, the two imply that the disciple is nonresistant (takes off clothing) before the powers of the material world when they demand their own, the body; but he resists (binds on clothing) when the world and its powers seek what is not their own, the soul (cf. *Ep. Pet. Phil.* [NHC 8, 2] 137.25–27). The story of the householder and thief seems to have been added after that of the children in the field as a counterstory to interpret the first.

Now we can explain why the saying about treading on a garment has become a story (21a). The structure for the story is borrowed from the parable of the house-

these logia was similar to that in the *Gospel of the Egyptians.* Did the authors of these three documents know the Dominical Saying independently from oral tradition or were they literarily interdependent? The very fact that they come from Egypt, Greece, and Syria suggests that the relationship is oral not literary. Lore, being lighter, travels faster than letter. Furthermore, the *Gospel of Thomas* almost certainly knew nothing of *2 Clement* and seems not to have known the *Gospel of the Egyptians.* The *Gospel of the Egyptians* apparently did not know the *Gospel of Thomas* or *2 Clement.* However, several scholars have suggested that the preacher of *2 Clement* knew the *Gospel of the Egyptians.* One can decide this matter only by comparing the citations of the Dominical Saying; the three other extracanonical sayings of Jesus quoted in *2 Clement* cannot be attributed to this gospel.[12] A careful examination suggests that the preacher quoted the saying either from a written source other than the *Gospel of the Egyptians* or, more likely, from oral tradition.[13]

Although the saying appears in three quite different versions, its underlying structure remains sturdy throughout, as one can see from the following synopsis.

---

holder and thief. By patterning the story of the children in the field after that of the householder and thief, the evangelist skillfully expressed the disciple's tenuous relationship to the material world but tenacious attitude to the welfare of the soul. The garment image in the second story is the only element of it which could not have come from Q (or Matthew or Luke), and it is the only element of the story that "when you tread upon the garment of shame" could have provided.

Direct appeals to the reader such as we find in 21c are common in this gospel. For example, "Let him who has ears to hear hear" appears also in logia 8, 63, 65, and 96. This section with its saying about the sickle (cf. Mark 4:29) and "Let him who has ears to hear hear" seems to have been added to challenge the reader to grasp the secret meaning; in this case, the meaning hidden in the comparison of the two allegories. The only other element separating the garment allegory from "when the two become one," etc. is 22a: "Jesus saw some children taking milk. He said to this disciples, 'These children who are taking milk are like those who have entered the Kingdom.' They said to him, 'Shall we then, being children, enter the Kingdom?'" Instead of separating the tradition, however, this introduction to the two-becoming-one passage ties it together with the garment passage, for in 21a Mary's question, "Whom are your disciples like?," was answered, "They are like little children." Even though the evangelist separated the two sections of the tradition such as we find it in the *Gospel of the Egyptians,* he tied the major elements together again by references to the disciples as children.

[12] These other agrapha appear in *2 Clem.* 4.5; 5.2–4; and 13.2.
[13] See Lightfoot, *Apostolic Fathers,* 1. 2. p. 236, n. 14.

Gos. Eg.	2 Clement	Gos. Thom. 21a and 22	Gos. Thom. 37
The Lord said	The Lord said	He said, "They are like little children who dwell in a field not theirs.	Jesus said,
"When (ὅταν)		When (ⲍⲟⲧⲁⲛ) the masters of the field come they will say, 'Give our field to us.'	"When (ⲍⲟⲧⲁⲛ)
on the garment of shame		They take off (their garments) before them,	you take off your shame and take your garments and put them under your feet like these little children
you tread,			and tread on them. ..."
		to release it to them and to give back their field to them. ...."	
and when (ὅταν) the two become one,	When (ὅταν) the two become one,	"When (ⲍⲟⲧⲁⲛ) you make the two one, and you make the inside as the outside,	
	and the outside as the inside	and the outside as the inside, and the above as the below.	
and the male with the female	and the male with the female	and when you make the male with the female into a single one, so that	
neither male nor female."	neither male nor female ...	the male will not be male and the female not be female. When you make eyes in the place of an eye, and a hand in the place of a hand, and a foot in the place of a foot— an image in the place of an image— then you shall enter	
	when you have done these things the Kingdom will come."	the Kingdom."	

Later in this chapter we shall see why authors of these three documents altered the saying as they did, but for now it is sufficient to observe what they have in common. In each instance, Jesus is asked about the future and he responds with a statement in the form of ὅταν/ⲌⲞⲦⲀⲚ ("when") and a verb in the second person plural— even in the *Gospel of the Egyptians* and *2 Clement* where the inquirer is an individual. In two of the citations we find a reference to treading on a garment of shame. Next come lists of opposites which the tradition expanded liberally. In each case, however, the lists begin with ὅταν/ *hotan,* the two becoming one, and end with "the male with the female neither male nor female." In the *Gospel of the Egyptians* and *2 Clement* the verbs in the lists are third person singular, even though the quotation in the former begins in the second person plural. In both *2 Clement* and *Gos. Thom.* 22 the saying ends with a reference to "the kingdom." It would therefore appear that in the most stabile version of the saying now detectable, Jesus answers his interlocutor by saying:

> ὅταν τὸ τῆς αἰσχύνης ἔνδυμα πατήσητε, καὶ ὅταν γένηται (or ἔσται) τὰ δύο ἕν, καὶ τὸ ἔξω ὡς τὸ ἔσω, καὶ τὸ ἄρσεν μετὰ τῆς θηλείας οὔτε ἄρσεν καὶ θῆλυ τότε . . . ἡ βασιλεία.

> When you tread upon the garment of shame, and when the two become one, and the outside as the inside, and the male with the female neither male nor female, then . . . the Kingdom.

Each of the elements that make this Dominical Saying and Gal 3:26-28 most similar persists in at least two of the three versions: a garment allusion in the second person plural, the two becoming one, the change of person to the third singular, and "neither male nor female."

2.2 The Meaning of the Saying

The images of putting off garments and of making the two one have a long history in anthropological discussions among Greek philosophers. Documents from the Orphic/Platonic tradition frequently speak of the captivity of the soul in matter as the result of its "putting on" the body. The earliest use of the metaphor appears in a fragment of Empedocles (5th c. BCE), "(A female divinity) clothing

(the soul) in the unfamiliar tunic of flesh,"[14] and it became philosophical commonplace in later Platonic tradition.[15] Consequently, the
soul achieves its ideal state when it removes its bodily garment.
According to Plato, souls after death must leave their fleshly bodies
"strewn upon the earth" before ascending to judgment.[16] But even
before death the soul of a philosopher can detach itself from the
body,[17] insofar as she recognizes the soul's true nature and practices
death to the body.[18] Plotinus too speaks of the philosopher's mystical
transport as "stripping off the garments with which we were clothed
when we descended from mind and reascending in our naked
selves."[19]

Also popular in this philosophical tradition was the metaphor of
the "two becoming one." Oneness symbolized perfection; duality or
"the many" imperfection. Frequently in Plato, "the one" stood for
the idea or form; "the many" for the idea's actual condition in
matter—one idea of turtle; many turtles. In the *Symposium*, however, the two that become one are the two sexes desiring to reunite
themselves into primordial unity. (We shall have more to say about
this later.) In Plotinus, the soul of the philosopher unites with the
One by means of mystical reflection, and this is often couched in the
love imagery of the *Symposium*.

> The soul sees God suddenly appearing within it, because there is
> nothing between: they are no longer two, but one; while the
> presence lasts, you cannot distinguish them. It is that union
> which earthly lovers imitate when they would be one flesh. The
> soul is no longer conscious of being in a body.[20]

---

[14] Empedocles, frg. 126 in Hermann Diels, *Die Fragmente der Vorsokratiker* (4th ed.;
Berlin: Weidmann, 1922).

[15] See, e.g., John M. Rist's discussion ("A Common Metaphor," *Plotinus: The Road
to Reality* [Cambridge: Cambridge University Press, 1967] 188–98) of the imagery in
later Platonists. To Rist's examples we may add Maximus of Tyre 2.10b, 11e; Proclus
Institutio theologica prop. 209; and Porphyry *De abstinentia* 1.31, 2.46.

[16] *Gorgias* 523.

[17] *Phaedo* 67c, 82–83; *Gorgias* 493a; and *Meno* 64e–65a.

[18] *Phaedo* 80–81.

[19] *Ennead* 1.6.7.5–7 (as quoted in Rist, *Plotinus*, 188). For an excellent overview of
this garment imagery in the history of religions see Meeks, "Image of the Androgyne," 187–89.

[20] *Ennead* 6.7.34.12ff. (as quoted in E. R. Dodds, *Pagan and Christian in an Age of
Anxiety: Some Aspects of Religious Experience from Marcus Aurelius to Constantine* [New
York: Norton, 1970] 85–86). See also *Ennead* 6.9–11.

Common to these various interpretations is the notion that life in this world is characterized by division, whether of the multiplication of ideas in the phenomenal world, the division of the sexes, or the separation of the individual soul from the One. Each interpretation also speaks of a reuniting in ontological terms: as the return to the single idea from which "the many" came, as the reunification of the sexes into their primordial oneness, or as the soul's ascent to the One.

It is within the context of this philosophical tradition and its religious permutations in hellenized Judaism and Gnosticism that we should interpret the imagery of the Dominical Saying. "The garment of shame" referred to the human body on which one must trample in order to make the outside, the soul's material "garment," like the inside, the soul itself. "When the two become one" refers, as in the *Symposium*, to the two sexes returning to their primordial unity, thereby making the believer "neither male nor female."[21]

---

[21] This basic anthropogony is older than Empedocles, who said the world once was ruled by the power of unification or Love (*philia*). This was a golden age when all animals were gentle toward people (B.130), warfare and animal sacrifice were unknown, and the gods of violence (Zeus, Cronos, Poseidon, and Ares) had not yet been born (B.128). Love held together the two sexes into a single creature, "mixed in part from man, in part of female sex, furnished with hairy limbs" (B.61; as translated by Kathleen Freeman, *Ancilla to the Pre-Socratic Philosophers* [Cambridge: Harvard University Press, 1977] 59). They were giants who used these limbs to do cartwheels, for they were "creatures with rolling gait and innumerable hands" (A.77, B.60; Freeman, p. 58). During this golden reign of Love, Empedocles himself in primordial preexistence was in the company of the gods, plotting with Hate to overthrow Love. Apparently, Hate successfully ousted Love from her control of the world. Hate unleashed vices, created antipathy between animals and humans, and divided the giant androgynes into male and females. Trees only have retained their androgyny (A.70). Sexual desire is one sex seeing the other and longing for reunification (B.64). Thus did Hate rule the world, but Love continued to rule heaven. Consequently, Love punished Empedocles for his complicity with Hate and sent him away as "a fugitive from heaven," banned from the gods for thirty thousand seasons (B.115; Freeman, p. 65).

He describes his descent into the world as a descent into a "roofed cavern" (B.120), a "joyless land where are Murder and Wrath and the tribes of other Dooms" (B.121; Freeman, p. 65). During his descent a female divinity clothed his soul "in the foreign tunic of flesh" (B.126) for the body is "earth that envelops mortals" (B.148). At his birth he "wept and wailed when he saw the foreign land" (B.118; Freeman, p. 65). His mission in his present incarnation (he already had been a boy, a girl, a plant, a bird, and a fish; B.117) was to communicate to mortals the true nature of things: "Alas, oh wretched race of mortals, direly unblessed! Such are the conflicts and grownings from which you have been born!" (B.124; Freeman, p. 66).

There is, however, hope for the soul that submits to purifications (hence the title of the poem, *Purifications*). "Souls are divine, and also divine are those who keep

The best example of this religious anthropology among Jews comes from the interpretations on Genesis written by Philo of Alexandria, a Jewish middle platonic philosopher. According to Philo, the two creation stories in Genesis (1:1-2:4a and 2:4b-3:24) tell of two successive stages of creation. The first speaks of a human made in God's image (1:26-27), the second of a human molded out of the dust of the earth (2:7). Thus,

> there are two types of humans: the one a heavenly human, the other an earthly. The heavenly human being made after the image of God, is altogether without part or lot in corruptible and terrestial substance; but the earthly was compacted out of matter scattered here and there, which Moses calls "clay." For this reason he says the heavenly human was not moulded (πεπλάσθαι) but was stamped with the image of God (κατ' εἰκόνα δὲ τετυπῶσθαι θεοῦ); while the earthly is a moulded work of the Artificer, but not His offspring.[22]

---

themselves pure" (A.32; translation mine). When the soul recognizes its essential alienation from the body it can serve the principle of unification and proceed to apotheosis by right thinking and acting. That is, one must think rightly about God, who is "Mind, holy and ineffable, and only Mind, which darts through the whole universe with its swift thoughts" (B.134). Furthermore, one must abstain from animal sacrifices, avoid laurel leaves and beans, "fast from sin," practice celibacy, and observe rites of diverting water with one's hands from five springs into a vessel of bronze (B.136, 137, 140, 141, 143, 144). By so doing individuals can become "seers, and bards, and physicians, and princes," and ultimately can "blossom forth as gods" (B.146; Freeman, p. 68), "sharing the hearth of the other immortals, sharing the same table freed from the lot of human griefs" (B.147; Freeman, p. 68).

It is difficult to know how much of Empedocles' teaching was original and how much traditional. Certainly elements of his ideas appear already in early Orphism and Pythagoreanism. But Empedocles is the earliest author from whom we can document this popular religious anthropology that profoundly influenced ancient Greek philosophy, Judaism, Christianity, and Gnosticism. Some early Christians believed that he was the sole origin for Gnostic ideas concerning the primal androgynous Adam and the soul's fall into the material world (Hippol. *Haer.* 5.2), for Simon Magus's statements concerning reincarnation or metempsychosis (Tert. *De anima* 32; cf. Hippol. *Haer.* 1.3; 4.6), and for Marcion's rival primordial powers—the evil creator god of the Jews, and the good god revealed by Jesus (Hippol. *Haer.* 7.17–19). But these claims are simply stock heresiological arguments intended to deprive ideas of credence by associating them with out-of-vogue philosophers. The residual truth in these charges is this: Empedocles did indeed express a cosmology and religious anthropology that flourished *mutatis mutandis* in Gnostic circles.

[22] *Leg. all.* 1.31.

Those who cultivate the life of the soul attempt to detach themselves from matter and thereby regain the image of God as exemplified by the first Adam.[23]

Philo saw in the second creation story a change in Adam's sexuality:

> He [God] makes it most clear that there is an immense difference between this moulded human and the one made previously after the image of God; for the moulded one is an object of sense, partaking already of quality consisting of body and soul, man or woman, mortal by nature; while that which was after the image was an idea or type or seal, an object of thought (only), incorporeal (ἀσώματος), neither male nor female (οὔτε ἄρρεν οὔτε θῆλυ), incorruptible by nature.[24]

Even the second Adam, "as long as he was one" (μέχρι ... εἷς ἦν), imitated unity (μόνωσις) with God and the universe.[25] His fall came with the division of the sexes: "woman becomes for him the beginning of a blameworthy life" inasmuch as desire was spawned from their longing to be one again.

> Love (ἔρως) supervenes, brings together and fits into one the divided halves, as it were, of a single living creature, and set up in each of them a desire for fellowship with the other with a view to the production of their like. And this desire begat likewise violation of law, the pleasure which is the beginning of wrongs and violation of law, the pleasure for the sake of which people bring on themselves the life of mortality and wretchedness in lieu of that immortality and bliss.[26]

The "coat of skins" with which God clothed the first couple was the skin of the body,[27] or the body itself.[28]

Accordingly, the soul finds salvation in a return to the state of the first human, in a liberation from the body, which Philo calls a

---

[23] *De plant.* 18–20; *De op. mun.* 134–35; *Leg. all.* 1.31, 33.
[24] *De op. mun.* 134; translation mine. See also *Leg. all.* 1.53, 88–92; *De plant.* 44; *Quis her.* 57; *Quest. Gen.* 1.4, 8; 2.56; and 4.160.
[25] *De op. mun.* 151.
[26] Ibid., 152.
[27] *Quest. Gen.* 1.53.
[28] Ibid., 4.78.

shell,[29] a tent,[30] a vessel which grows old and dissolves,[31] a foreign
country in which the lover of virtue sojourns,[32] a camp the mind
desires to leave to contemplate the incorporeal,[33] an ark one must
leave,[34] a hedge one must cross,[35] a tomb one must flee,[36] a building, a house or a prison from which one must be freed,[37] a corpse
one must condemn to death.[38]

One of Philo's favorite images for the body is the garment. For
example, the soul loving God, "having disrobed itself of the body
(ἐκδῦσα τὸ σῶμα) . . . fled far away."[39] "Our soul moves often by
itself, stripping itself of the entire encumbrance of the body (ὅλον τὸ
σωματικὸν ὄγκον ἐκδῦσα)."[40] On the other hand, "those who have
made a compact and a truce with the body are unable to cast off
from them the garment of flesh."[41]

Death is the separation of the soul, "the inside," from the body,
"the outside,"[42] whereby the soul returns to its place of origin.[43] But
this separation and flight of the soul also comes before death to
those who,

> descending into the body as though into a stream . . . have
> been able to stem the current, they have risen to the surface
> and then soared upwards back to the place whence they came.
> These . . . are the souls of those who have given themselves to
> genuine philosophy, who from first to last study to die to the life
> in the body.[44]

---

[29] *De Iosepho* 71.
[30] *Quest. Gen.* 4.11.
[31] *De som.* 1.26; *De mig.* 193; *Quod det.* 170.
[32] *Quis her.* 267.
[33] *De ebrietate* 99; cf. *Leg. all.* 3.46.
[34] *De conf.* 105; *Quest. Gen.* 2.114; *Quod det.* 170.
[35] *Quest. Gen.* 4.185.
[36] *Leg. all.* 1.108; *Quod Deus imm.* 150; cf. *Quest. Gen.* 1.70 and 4.75.
[37] *De conf.* 177; *Quest. Gen.* 4.94; *De som.* 1.122; *De praem.* 120-21; *Quod Deus imm.*
150; *De agric.* 25.
[38] *Leg. all.* 3.72-75; cf. 1.108, *Quest. Gen.* 1.93 and 2.12.
[39] *Leg. all.* 2.55, cf. 56.
[40] *De som.* 1.43. Cf. *De gig.* 53; *De mig.* 192; *De praem.* 166; and *Leg. all.* 57-58.
[41] *Quod Deus imm.* 56.
[42] For examples see *Leg. all.* 3.40-41; *De ebrietate* 147; and *Quis her.* 81-85.
[43] *De conf.* 78; *De Abrahamo* 258. See also *De sac.* 8-9; *De agric.* 65; *Leg. all.* 1.108;
De spec. leg. 3.207; *De cher.* 114; and *De virt.* 76-77.
[44] *De gig.* 13-14. See also *Quest. Gen.* 4.46, 138; *De Mos.* 1.279; *Quis her.* 29; *Leg.
all.* 3.71.

The mind becomes light as it proceeds to higher things where it can see unhindered the light of wisdom.[45] Thus the Therapeutae of Egypt, by contemplation, "have lived in the soul alone."[46] "The wise man, having a body that is inanimate and heavy, like a bronze statue, is always carrying a corpse."[47] In fact, "we may almost make it an axiom that the business of wisdom is to become estranged from the body and its cravings."[48] This estrangement from the body may also have happened in ritual or "mysteries" in which the mind transcends the body: "When the mind soars aloft and is being initiated into the mysteries of the Lord, it judges the body to be evil and hostile."[49]

In a detailed analysis of Philo's treatments of Genesis 1-3, Thomas H. Tobin argues that Philo inherited the notion of the two-staged creation of Adam from Alexandrian Jewish exegetical tradition.[50] The clearest proof of Tobin's thesis is *Quest. Gen.* 1.8, where Philo asks: "Why does he [God] place the molded man [i.e., the second Adam] in Paradise, but not the man who was made in his image?" Philo's answer reveals that the question was debated among previous interpreters who shared his view concerning the two creations of Adam:

> *Some*, believing Paradise to be a garden, have said that since the molded man is sense-perceptible, he therefore rightly goes to a sense-perceptible place. But the man made in his image is intel-

[45] *Quest. Gen.* 4.46, 193; and *De Mos.* 2.288: "Afterwards the time came when he [Moses] had to make his pilgrimage from earth to heaven, and leave this mortal life for immortality, summoned thither by the Father Who resolved his twofold nature of soul and body into a single unity, transforming his whole being into mind, pure as the sunlight."
[46] *De cont.* 90. See also *De Abrahamo* 236; *De sac.* 9–10; and *De agric.* 64–65.
[47] *Quest. Gen.* 4.77.
[48] *Leg. all.* 1.103. Cf. Plato *Phaedo* 65a: "In such matters the philosopher, more than other men, separates the soul from communion with the body." See also *Quod prob.* 107. Philo never tires of using allegories to speak of the soul's release: the separation of the soul is what is meant by Moses' taking his tent outside the camp (*Quod det.* 159–60), or by Abraham's leaving his land (*De mig.* 1–3 and *Quest. Gen.* 4.74), or by his sojourning in Egypt (*De conf.* 78–82), or by circumcision (*Quest. Gen.* 3.52) or by Noah's being "naked in his house" (*De plant.* 140–77).
[49] *Leg. all.* 3.71. The context speaks of the mind's wearing the body like a corpse from an allegory on Er, Judah's eldest son, whose name Philo says means "leathern." See also *De praem.* 121.
[50] Tobin, *The Creation of Man: Philo and the History of Interpretation* (CBQMS 14; Washington: The Catholic Biblical Association of America, 1983).

ligible and invisible. . . . *But I would say* that Paradise should be thought a symbol of wisdom."[51]

Nor was the double creation of Adam a notion unique to Alexandrian Jews; it thrived as well in second- and third-century Christianity and Gnosticism. For example, Irenaeus wrote that Gnostic Marcosians "hold that one man was formed after the image and likeness of God, masculo-feminine, and that this was the spiritual man; and that another was formed out of the earth."[52]

We shall now see that this exegetical merger of Platonic anthropological dualism with Genesis 1-3 provides the best conceptual background for the Dominical Saying, inasmuch as the images of the saying refer to the soul's liberation from matter and sexuality as it returns to the image of the heavenly Adam. In order to establish this as the proper understanding of the saying, we shall examine in some detail the interpretations of it provided by the *Gospel of the Egyptians*, Julius Cassianus, Clement of Alexandria, *2 Clement*, and the *Gospel of Thomas*.

The Gospel of the Egyptians

Even though only a few fragments of this gospel remain, it is possible to reconstruct its basic soteriology: salvation consists of a recapitulation of Adam's primordial state.

> Salome said, "How long will people die?" Jesus answered, "As long as women bear children."[53] And Salome said to him, "Then I have done well in not bearing children?" Jesus answered and said, "Eat every plant, but the plant which is bitter you shall not eat."[54]

From its similarity with Gen 2:16–17a it is clear this last sentence alludes to the prohibition of the tree of knowledge understood as sexual intercourse.[55] By refraining from sex, Salome can end the

---

[51] See Tobin, *Creation*, 32–33, 108–34, 172–74.

[52] Iren. *Adv. haer.* 1.18.2.

[53] Clem. Al. *Strom.* 3.9.64. This saying, slightly altered, occurs also in 3.6.45 and *Exc. Theod.* 67.

[54] Clem. Al. *Strom.* 3.9.66. Clement explicitly says these two sayings appeared together in this order.

[55] Notice the similarities between the prohibition of the bitter plant and the prohibition of the tree of knowledge in Genesis:

cycle of birth and death. Perhaps we should interpret the following passage also in the context of sexual asceticism: Jesus said, "I have come to destroy the works of the female."[56]
The only other fragment of the gospel to have come down to us is the Dominical Saying.

When Salome asked when the events about which she inquired would be known the Lord said: "When you tread upon the garment of shame, and when the two are one, and the male with the female neither male nor female."[57]

In light of the other passages of this gospel it would seem wisest to assume that the "garment of shame" refers to the "coats of skins" God gave the first couple to cover their shame.[58] Behind the "two are one" might be Gen 2:24, "The two will become one flesh."

Gos. Eg.	Gen 2:16–17a (LXX)
πᾶσαν φάγε βοτάνην	ἀπὸ πάντος ξύλου . . . φάγῃ
τὴν δὲ πικρίαν ἔχουσαν	ἀπὸ δὲ ξύλου τοῦ γινώσκειν
μὴ φάγῃς.	οὐ φάγεσθε.

The book *Baruch* (Hippol. *Haer.* 5.26.22–23) and Julius Cassianus (Clem. Al. *Strom.* 3.17.104) both interpeted the eating of the tree of knowledge as intercourse. This probably also is the meaning of *Acts of Peter* 8 where Peter tells the Devil: "Thou hast ensnared the first man in lustful desire and bound him to thine ancient wickedness and with the chain of the body; thou art the fruit of the tree of bitterness, which is most bitter, inducing lusts of every kind" (*NTApoc*, 2. 290). See also *Gos. Phil.* (NHC 2, 3) 71.22–34; *Acts Thom.* 44; *Acts Andr.* (Vaticanus graecus 808) 5; *Gos Thom.* 40; and *Odes Sol.* 11:21. Jean-Paul Broudéhoux agrees with this interpretation of the *Gospel of the Egyptians* (*Mariage et famille chez Clément d'Alexandrie* [ThH 2; Paris: Beauchesne, 1970] 55).
As Clement himself recognized (*Strom.* 3.17.104), this interpretation depends on a double entendre for γινώσκω. In the LXX it is used to translate *yada'* in both of its meanings: "to know," and "to know sexually." So for instance, in Genesis 2–3 Adam and Eve eat of τὸ ξύλον τοῦ γινώσκειν and after they are expelled from the garden the LXX reads Αδαμ δὲ ἔγνω Ευαν . . . καὶ συλλαβοῦσα ἔτεκεν τὸν Καιν (Gen 4:1).
[56] Clem. Al. *Strom.* 3.9.63. The *Second Treatise of the Great Seth* says, "Do not become female, lest you give birth to evil and (its) brothers" ([NHC 7, 2] 65.24–25). In the *Dialogue of the Savior* the Lord commands: "Pray in the place where there is no woman, (and) destroy the works of femaleness" ([NHC 3, 5] 144.18–20).
[57] Clem. Al. *Strom.* 3.13.92.
[58] Gilles Quispel writes: "Das Fragment des Aegypterevangelium: ὅταν τὸ τῆς αἰσχύνης ἔνδυμα πατήσητε setze dieselbe Interpretation von Genesis 3:21 voraus"; i.e., the same interpretation as in the "Hymn of the Pearl" ("Makarius und das Lied von der Perle," in Bianchi, ed., *Le origini dello gnosticismo*, 634).

Gen 1:27, "He made them male and female," may have informed "neither male and female." Compare the following:

Gos. Eg.	Gen 3:21 (LXX)
ὅταν τὸ τῆς αἰσχύνης ἔνδυμα πατήσητε,	καὶ ἐποίησεν κύριος ... χιτῶνας δερματίνους, καὶ ἐνέδυσεν αὐτούς.
	Gen 2:24–25
καὶ ὅταν γένηται τὰ δύο ἕν,	καὶ ἔσονται οἱ δύο εἰς σάρκα μίαν, καὶ ἦσαν οἱ δύο γυμνοί, ὅ τε Ἀδὰμ καὶ ἡ γυνὴ αὐτοῦ, καὶ οὐκ ᾐσχύνοντο.
	Gen 1:27
καὶ τὸ ἄρρεν μετὰ τῆς θηλείας οὔτε ἄρρεν οὔτε θῆλυ.	ἄρσεν καὶ θῆλυ ἐποίησεν αὐτούς.

Even though little more can be said about the meaning of this saying from the *Gospel of the Egyptians,* we can reconstruct—with difficulty but with relative confidence—the theology and Genesis speculations of some of its principal users, Julius Cassianus and his circle of ascetics.

Julius Cassianus

The difficulty in understanding Julius Cassianus stems from the condition of our witnesses to him. Of his life we know only that he was a rigorous ascetic, from the "school of Valentinus," and the leader (ἔξαρχος) of the Docetists.[59] He wrote a multi-volume work of biblical interpretation, *Exegetics*—the first book of which Clement of Alexandria lauded as an accurate account of the antiquity of

---

[59] Clem. Al. *Strom.* 3.13.91. Adolph Hilgenfeld (*Die Ketzergeschichte des Urchristentums* [Leipzig: Fues, 1884] 546–49) interprets ἔξαρχος to mean the founder of Docetism, but Jean-Paul Broudéhoux no doubt is correct when he writes: "Docetism was in existence well before Cassianus, and nothing permits one any longer to believe that Cassianus had founded a sect of 'Docetists'" (*Mariage et famille,* 57).

Hebrew philosophy[60]—and a work *On Continence* or *On Eunuchism*, which seems to have been a topical exposition of biblical texts.[61] All that remains of these are a few scraps used to make Clement's "quilt," his *Stromateis*.[62] If we are to reconstruct Cassianus's theological design, we must first collect these scraps and piece them together. Clement referred to Cassianus explicitly only in *Strom.* 3.13.91–17.104, but it is clear that the section immediately preceding it should also be connected with him.[63] Furthermore, in 3.6.45–50 and 9.63–66 Clement opposed a theology identical to that of Cassianus.[64] Our interpretation of Cassianus then will be limited to *Strom.* 3.6.45–50; 9.63–66; and 12.86–17.104. Furthermore, we shall discuss only those aspects of his theology germane to understanding how he understood the Dominical Saying.

A. The Garment of Shame

Clement (*Strom.* 3.13.93) accused Cassianus of interpreting the Dominical Saying "platonically"; that is, by means of Platonic psychology. Presumably Clement had in mind passages like *Phaedrus* 248c or *Phaedo* 81c in which souls are said to have fallen into the material world because of their desire for the corporeal. But he also might have been thinking of *Timaeus* 42a–d, where the soul of the wicked is changed into a woman's nature at the second birth and remains separated from her native star until she repents. Then she puts off her body and returns to her "first and best state," her heavenly abode. Regardless of which passage Clement had in mind, Cassianus found this fall of the soul in Paul as well: "I am afraid that, as the serpent deceived Eve, your minds will be corrupted from

---

[60] Clem. Al. *Strom.* 1.21.101.

[61] Clem. Al. *Strom.* 3.13.

[62] Cassianus is also mentioned in Theodoret (*Haereticarum fabularum compendium* 1.8), and Jerome claims that Cassianus used Gal 6:8 to support his asceticism (see Hilgenfeld, *Ketzergeschichte*, 546–49).

[63] *Strom.* 3.12.86–90. This identification is indicated by Clement himself when he introduces Cassianus in 3.13.91 with the words τοιούτοις ἐπιχειρεῖ καὶ ὁ ... Ἰούλιος Κασσιανός. See also Edward Schwartz, *Tatiani Oratio ad Graecos* (TU 4, 1; Leipzig: Hinrichs, 1888) 49 for dividing 80–86a, on Tatian, from 86b.

[64] Franco Bolgiani, "La polemica di Clemente Alessandrino contro gli libertini nel III libro degli 'Stromati,'" in *Studi in onore di Alberto Pincherle* (Studi e materiali de storia delle religioni 38, 1; Rome: Ateneo, 1967) 93–94.

the singleness (ἁπλότης) with reference to Christ."[65] The mind or soul, Cassianus claimed, was corrupted by deception and left its primordial heavenly singleness, which he might have understood as its androgyny.[66]

The primary source for Cassianus's interpretation was neither Plato nor Paul, but Genesis 1–3, just as it had been for the *Gospel of the Egyptians*. The fall of the soul into the world, according to Cassianus, was the result of the deception of our first parents when they ate of the forbidden tree—that is, when Adam and Eve enjoyed the sexual union the serpent had learned from the animals.[67] For this transgression they were incarcerated in mortal bodies; God clothed them in "coats of skins."[68] By dint of their union and procreation, other souls have strayed and become enslaved in bodies.[69]

Salvation is the soul's escape from her fleshy prison, not only at death, but also before death by "putting off the old human," and by "putting on the new human," that is, by recovering the primordial image of the immaterial God. One can see this soteriology at work behind Clement's elliptical discussion of Cassianus's use of Eph 4:22–24, the command to "put off the old human which belongs to the former way of living, corrupted through the desires of deceit . . . and put on the new human created (κτισθέντα—Clement reads κτιζόμενον) after God." Clement's argument goes like this:

> When the apostle says "put on the new human who is being created in God's image," he tells us who have been molded that we have already been molded by the will of the Almighty, and

[65] *Strom.* 3.14.94, quoting 2 Cor 11:3.

[66] 68. Perhaps there is a suggestion of the loss of androgyny in Cassianus's use of 2 Cor 11:3, which originally was in the context of *hieros gamos* imagery: "I feel a divine jealousy for you, for I betrothed you to Christ, to present you as a pure bride to her one husband, but I fear that, as the serpent deceived Eve, your thoughts will be corrupted from the singleness (ἁπλότητος) with reference to Christ." Of course, ἁπλότης can also be translated "simplicity"—as it should for Paul's intention—but perhaps the reading "singleness" is better for understanding Cassianus's use of it. He interpreted this text as proof that the soul or mind was deceived by the serpent to leave heaven and come to birth. The "singleness with reference to Christ" in that case might well refer to the soul's natural sexual unity.

[67] *Strom.* 3.17.102, 104. "The phrase 'he knew' (ἔγνω, Gen 4:1) signifies the transgression of the commandment."

[68] *Strom.* 3.14.95.

[69] To support the relationship between the curses of the fall and birth he quoted Isa 65:23: "My elect will not labor in vain, nor will they bear children for a curse, for there is a seed blessed by the Lord" (*Strom.* 3.15.98); and Jer 20:14: "Cursed be the day in which I was born and let it not be sought for" (3.16.100).

he does not speak of the old (and the new) to represent birth
and rebirth, but the life of disobedience and (the life of) obedience. And Cassianus thinks the "coats of skins" are bodies.[70]
(translation mine)

Apparently behind Clement's argument lies a distinction between
two kinds of humanity. Philo and others attached great importance
to the distinction between God's creating (κτίζω), or making
(ποιέω, Gen 1:27 LXX) Adam and God's molding (πλάσσω, Gen
2:7 LXX) him.[71] Philo said, "The human whom God made
(ἐποίησεν) differs . . . from the one that 'was molded' (τοῦ
πλασθέντος): for the one that was made is less material, having no
part in perishable matter."[72] A similar distinction informs
Cassianus's soteriology. The "old human . . . corrupted through the
desires of deceit" was the body, the result of having been molded
from dust, of Eve's seduction, and of physical birth. The body was
the coat of skin given the first pair which one must put off. To "put
on the new human created after God" was to be reborn to the original primordial condition. Cassianus could also speak of this rebirth
as a *re*molding: "The Lord remolded (μετέπλασεν) us and delivered
us from the fellowship of genitalia and appendages."[73]

Against Cassianus Clement argued that the original molding of the
human body was by divine design, not a result of the soul's sin or a
demiurge's blunder. One does not need a rebirth or a remolding to a
new ontological condition; one needs a life of obedience which will
result in a new moral condition. For him, "putting on the new
human" was the result of a moral process, not the result of a cultic
act or a mystical experience.[74]

But for Cassianus, the believer already had put off the body,
because he or she already had been raised to be with Christ. In
Strom. 3.6.47–48 Clement quoted Matt 22:30: "After the

---

[70] *Strom.* 3.14.95.

[71] See Birger A. Pearson, *The Pneumatikos-Psychikos Terminology* (SBLDS; Missoula:
Scholars Press, 1973) 15–16, 51–81.

[72] *Leg. all.* 1.88; cf. 4.31.

[73] *Strom.* 3.13.92.

[74] This may explain the alteration of κτισθέντα to κτιζόμενον in Clement's quotation of Eph 4:24. κτισθέντα is not only the best reading of the verse, it is also the
only reading Clement himself used every other time he quoted it (*Paid.* 3.3.17; *Strom.*
1.18.90; 3.4.28; and *Exc. Theod.* 19). Clement argues here that "putting on the new
human" is the result of a process, not a sacramental or mystical return to the perfect
condition. With this interpretation the present participle is more congenial than the
aorist.

resurrection they neither marry nor are given in marriage," in order
to prove that the Lord approved of marriage in the present age. But
his opponents claimed they had already attained the resurrection, and
for this reason they did not marry.[75] Theirs was a resurrection from
corporeality and its demands: sexual intercourse, childbirth, and
death.[76] Perhaps this resurrection is what Cassianus alluded to when
he said, "Those being ruled by earthly (kings) both give birth and
are born, but our government (πολίτευμα) is in heaven (cf. Phil
3:20), whence we also await a savior."[77] Treading on the garment of
shame was the *ante mortem* release of the soul from the body.

B. *The Two Are One*

As mentioned above, Clement accuses Cassianus of interpreting
the Dominical Saying platonically in that Cassianus claimed the "soul
is of divine origin and, having become female by desire, has come
down here from above to birth and corruption."[78] This reference to
the sexuality of the soul is essential for understanding Cassianus's
interpretation of "when the two are one and the male with the
female neither male nor female." Apparently behind his interpretation lay a myth of the soul's female fall. One indeed does find this
in Plato (e.g., *Timaeus* 42a–d), but it also appears in the *Exegesis on
the Soul*, a Coptic Nag Hammadi document apparently from Valentinian circles—like Cassianus himself. According to this document:
"As long as she [ΨΥΧΗ, Soul] was alone with the Father, she was
virgin and in form androgynous. But when she fell down into a body
and came to this life, then she fell into the hands of many
robbers."[79] In her fallen state, the soul is wholly female and sleeps
with her earthly paramours without satisfaction. She is saved by
repentance and the sacraments of baptism and the bridal chamber

[75] The Lucan version of this synoptic logion had a significant role to play in early
Christian conversations on sexuality (Luke 20:34–35). See, e.g., Clem. Al. *Strom.*
3.12.87. For a brief discussion see Arthur Vööbus, *The History of Asceticism in the
Syrian Orient; A Contribution to Culture in the Near East* (CSCO 184; Louvain:
Secrétariat du Corpus SCO, 1958) 1. 42–43.

[76] Clement (*Strom.* 3.6.48) complains that if they are truly resurrected they ought
not bother with eating and drinking.

[77] *Strom.* 3.14.95. Broudéhoux (*Mariage et famille*, 49) also relates this text to the
claim already to have been raised.

[78] *Strom.* 3.13.92.

[79] (NHC 2, 6) 127.22–27.

which return her to her former condition through a reunion with her bridegroom, her abandoned heavenly brother.

> And so the cleansing of the soul is to regain the [newness] of her former nature and to turn herself back again. That is her baptism.[80]
>
> But [once] they unite [with one another], they become a single life. Wherefore the prophet said (Gen 2:24) concerning the first man and the first woman, "They will become a single flesh." For they were originally joined to one another when they were with the Father before the woman led astray the man, who is her brother. This marriage has brought them back together again and the soul has been joined to her true love.[81]

The ultimate goal of the soul is that "she might be restored to the place where originally she had been. This is the resurrection that is from the dead. This is the ransom from captivity. This is the upward journey of ascent to heaven."[82]

In spite of differences in detail, one sees at once the similarities between these passages and Cassianus. Most important for us is the interpretation here of Gen 2:24b, "the two shall become one flesh." According to the *Exegesis on the Soul*, the soul originally was one-half of a heavenly androgyne. In the Greek world, the myth of the primordial androgyne was at least as old as Empedocles,[83] but it was given coin for the Hellenistic world by Plato's *Symposium*, even though Plato himself debunked the idea. Here, Aristophanes explains love (ἔρως) by claiming the first mortals had four legs, four arms, two heads, and were of three sexes: male/male, female/female, and male/female (ἀνδρόγυνον). For their hybris Zeus had Apollo divide them. What humans call love, therefore, is nothing other than the divided halves longing to be reunited, "to make one out of two."[84] The phrase "the two will become one

---

[80] Ibid. 131.34–132.2.

[81] Ibid. 132.34–133.9.

[82] Ibid. 134.10–14.

[83] Frgs. 61–62.

[84] *Symposium* 191d: ποιῆσαι ἓν ἐκ δυοῖν; and 192e: ἐκ δυοῖν εἰς γενέσθαι. It is worth noting that Philo, bemoaning the loss of Adam's unity, also speaks of ἔρως as the longing for reunification: "Eros supervenes, brings together and fits into one the divided halves, as it were, of a single living creature" (*De op. mun.* 152). For a more detailed discussion of the androgyne in Greco-Roman antiquity see Ernst Ludwig Dietrich, "Der Urmensch als Androgyn," *ZKG* 53 (1939) 297–345; Marie Delcourt, *Hermaphrodite, mythes et rites de la bisexualité dans l'antiquité classique* (Paris: Presses

flesh" in Gen 2:24 was similarly taken to be a return to primordial sexual oneness by those who thought Adam was an androgyne.[85] Although we are not told explicitly by Clement that Cassianus thought Adam had been an androgyne, it is quite likely he did. Like the *Exegesis on the Soul,* Cassianus (1) came from Valentinian circles, (2) thought of the soul as having become female in its fall into the world, and (3) preached celibacy as the behavioral result of returning to the primordial condition. It is reasonable to assume, therefore, that he thought the Dominical Saying required the soul's removal of the material body and the two sexes' again becoming one, that is, the female soul again becoming joined to her heavenly male counterpart. Since one experienced this "resurrection" before death, perhaps by a sacrament as in the *Exegesis on the Soul,* sexual relations were precluded. When the male was with the female they no longer responded as male and female.

Clement of Alexandria

Against Cassianus's use of the Dominical Saying, Clement at first devalues the saying as noncanonical, but then makes it congenial to his own theology.

> It speaks in enigmas of the male urge as wrath and the female lust. Whenever these are done repentance and shame follow. Therefore when someone does something neither in wrath or

---

universitaires de France, 1958); and idem, *Hermaphroditea, Recherchés sur l'être double promoteur de la fertilité dans le monde classique* (Collection Latomus; Bruxelles: Latomus, 1966). See also Derwood C. Smith, "The Two Made One: Some Observations on Ephesians 2:14–18," *Ohio Journal of Religious Studies* 1 (1973) 36–41.

[85] The belief that Adam was an androgyne was extremely widespread. *Berešith Rabbah* (VIII, 1 in *Midrash Rabbah* [trans. and ed. Rabbi H. Friedman and Maurice Simon; 13 vols. in 10; London: Soncino, 1939] 1. 54) says: "R. Jeremiah b. Leazar said:

> When the Holy One, blessed be He, created Adam, He created him an hermaphrodite, for it is said "Male and female created He them and called their name Adam"(Gen 5:2).

R. Samuel b. Nahman said:

> When the Lord created Adam He created him double-faced, then He split him and made him of two backs, one back on this side and one back on the other side.

See also Jervell, *Imago Dei,* 107–12; and Str-B 1. 802 and 4. 405–7. Adam's androgyny was also affirmed by Naassenes (Hippol. *Haer.* 5.1), by *The Gospel of Philip* ([NHC 2, 3] 68.22–26), and by *The Apocalypse of Adam* ([NHC 5, 5] 64.5–28).

lust (which indeed . . . overshadow and cover rationality [λογισμόν]) but takes off (ἀποδυσάμενοι) the mist of these things by repentance after having been made ashamed, he ought to unite spirit and soul by obedience to the Word [Λόγον]. Then, as Paul says "there is not among you a male nor a female." For by avoiding this form in which the male and female are distinguished, the soul changes into a unity, being neither of the two.[86]

The "garment of shame" is the "mist" of wrath and lust which covers rationality. One takes it off in repentance and shame. The "two become one" when the spirit and soul unite through obedience to the Word. The "male" (wrath) and the "female" (lust) are abolished when the soul leaves the form determined by these vices and becomes a unity.[87]

Here and in his refutation of Cassianus's use of Eph 4:2–24 Clement rejected the equation garment = body because the world and the body had been created according to God's will. Truly shameful were the passions, which clouded rationality (λογισμός) and thereby hindered obedience to the Word (Λόγος). His dependence on the pervasive middle Platonic tradition is obvious, since ethics for the Stoic presupposed a relationship between the human λογισμός and the divine Λόγος. The obedience of the will to the cosmic design was as close as the Stoic could come to the divine likeness. For Cassianus, the soul had been incarcerated in the body through a process of corruption (i.e., birth), but it could be saved by being reborn to its original perfection. But for Clement, God had originally created both soul and body, and in spite of their corruption by evil passions, humans could attain salvation through a process of obedience.

2 Clement

The citation of the Dominical Saying in *2 Clement* is very much like that in the *Gospel of the Egyptians*:

---

[86] *Strom.* 3.13.93.
[87] Compare Philo's psychologizing of sexual references in the Bible. See Richard A. Baer, *Philo's Use of the Categories Male and Female* (ALGHJ 3; Leiden: Brill, 1970).

Gospel of the Egyptians	*2 Clement*
When Salome inquired	For the Lord himself, when asked by someone (ὑπό τινος)
when (πότε) the things about which she asked would be known the Lord said: "When (ὅταν) you tread upon the garment of shame, and when (ὅταν) the two become one (γένηται τὰ δύο ἕν)	when (πότε) his Kingdom will come, said: "When (ὅταν) the two are one, (ἔσται τὰ δύο ἕν) and the outside as the inside,
and the male with the female neither male nor female." (καὶ τὸ ἄρρεν μετὰ τῆς θηλείας οὔτε ἄρρεν οὔτε θῆλυ)	and male with the female neither male nor female. . . . (καὶ τὸ ἄρσεν μετὰ τῆς θηλείας οὔτε ἄρσεν οὔτε θῆλυ) When you have done these things the Kingdom of my Father will come."

Was the preacher quoting from the *Gospel of the Egyptians*?[88] There is no reason whatever to think the preacher knew of this gospel apart from this one parallel. Only by comparing the two citations of the Dominical Saying can we determine their interrelationship.

"When you tread upon the garment of shame" is missing in *2 Clement*, but it is difficult to know whether or not it was in the source. Even if it were, the preacher might not have used it because of the widespread use of garment imagery to refer to the body. The preacher, for whom the body was not something to be trampled on but to be raised at the resurrection,[89] might have deleted the phrase to avoid its docetic implication.

---

[88] Of course it is theoretically possible that the *Gospel of the Egyptians* is dependent on *2 Clement*, but this is rendered unlikely by the inexplicable omission of "and the outside as the inside." Since we know that *2 Clement* elsewhere quoted Jesus traditions from several sources, and since we cannot isolate the use of traditional materials in the *Gospel of the Egyptians*, if there is any direct dependence of one on the other, it is more likely that *2 Clement* would have used the *Gospel of the Egyptians* than the other way around.

[89] *2 Clem.* 8.6; 9.1–5; 14.3, 5.

Certainly the source included "and the outside as the inside." It is unlikely Clement of Alexandria would have omitted this phrase had it been in the *Gospel of the Egyptians* inasmuch as he could have allegorized it as easily as he did the other elements of the saying. For example, he could have taken it to mean, as a good middle Platonist, that the body and its passions were to be as obedient to the Λόγος as the believer's ἡγεμονικόν or λογισμός were. It is also unlikely that Cassianus would have omitted it inasmuch as he could have taken it to mean the soul receives a new outside or body when it returns to the primordial incorporeal condition. It seems best then to assume the outside/inside clause was absent in the *Gospel of the Egyptians*,[90] and, if so, the preacher of *2 Clement* probably quoted from another source. Because of the radical theological differences between the Corinthian homily and the Egyptian gospel, we would also expect the preacher to have quoted the saying from oral tradition or from a written source with a theology more congenial with his own.[91]

This theological disagreement between the *Gospel of the Egyptians* and *2 Clement* is apparent in the latter's interpretation of the saying.

> Now "the two are one" when we speak with one another in truth, and there is but one soul in two bodies without dissimulation. And by "the outside as the inside" he means this, that the inside is the soul and the outside is the body. Therefore, just as your body is visible, so let your soul be apparent in good works. And by "the male with the female neither male nor female" he means this, that when a brother sees a sister he should have no thought of her as a female, nor she of him as a

---

[90] This absence of outside/inside in Clement's quotation of the *Gospel of the Egyptians* might be explained in several ways. It might have been already absent in the tradition used by the *Gospel of the Egyptians*, or it might have dropped out accidentally by haplography in the textual transmission (ὅταν ... καὶ ὅταν ... καὶ τὸ ... καὶ τὸ ...), or by redactional (or scribal) theological intention: by omitting that element, "when the two become one" is immediately followed by "and the male with the female neither male nor female." By this juxtapostion the two becoming one is more clearly taken to be the unification of the sexes. J. B. Lightfoot attributes this interpretative juxtaposition to Cassianus "who thus appears to have connected τὰ δύο ἕν closely with τὸ ἄρρεν μετὰ τῆς θηλείας and interpreted the expression similarly" (*Apostolic Fathers*, 1. 2. 238). No doubt Cassianus did interpret the two elements similarly, but it is not clear why he would have omitted a phrase so congenial to his soteriology.

[91] Helmut Koester agrees (*Synoptische Überlieferung bei den apostolischen Vätern* [TU 65; 5th ser. 10; Berlin: Akademie-Verlag, 1957] 103–5). See also Donfried, *Setting*, 77.

male. (*2 Clem.* 12.3-5; the translation is that of Kirsopp Lake, *The Apostolic Fathers* [LCL] 1. 147–49)

"The outside as the inside" is interpreted as though it read "the inside as the outside." The soul is to become like the body, apparent in its good works. This disagreement between the saying and its interpretation no doubt is responsible for the confusion in the textual witnesses,[92] and it radically alters the meaning of the phrase. For Cassianus and probably the *Gospel of the Egyptians* the body was to have become invisible like the soul, that is, the soul was to have acquired an immaterial outside; but for the preacher, the soul was to have become visible like the body. The goal of the first was escape from the material world; that of the second, escape from irrelevant spirituality. Like Clement of Alexandria, *2 Clement* interpreted the saying as moral paraenesis.

But unlike Clement, the preacher of *2 Clement* interpreted the male and the female as the human sexes, not as vices.[93] His exhortation that people not regard each other with respect to their sex need

---

[92] The textual witnesses widely disagree. The phrase occurs three times in *2 Clement*: (1) the original quotation of the saying, (2) a repetition of the phrase to be interpreted, and (3) again when it is interpreted.

Alexandrinus:
1. The outside as the inside
2. The outside as the inside
3. The soul is the inside and the body is the outside

Syriac:
1. The outside as the inside
2. The inside as the outside
3. The soul is the inside and the body is the outside

Constantinopolitanus:
1. The outside as the inside
2. The outside as the inside
3. The soul is the outside and the body is the inside

The original quotation is consistently "the outside as the inside." In the Syriac the second citation is "the inside as the outside" to conform to the author's interpretation, while Constantinopolitanus retains "the outside as the inside" throughout, thereby equating the soul with the outside and the body with the inside! (For the soul being on the outside see also Plato *Leg.* 10.898e and *Exeg. Soul* [NHC 2, 6] 131.16–34.)

[93] This is so even though his interpretation of Gen 1:27 makes "the male" Christ and "the female" the church (*2 Clem.* 14.2–5).

not imply sexual asceticism, although other sections of the homily suggest this may have been his intention.[94] More important than the preacher's interpretation of the tradition is his very use of it. Probably in Corinth at the beginning of the second century a preacher who defended the resurrection and value of the body used this saying in a sermon as though it were dominical. In the first half of the second century, then, the saying was used in Egypt and Greece by communities with competing theologies.

The Gospel of Thomas

A. *The Garment of Shame*

In the *Gospel of Thomas* we find a saying almost identical to the clause "when you tread upon the garment of shame" in the *Gospel of the Egyptians.*

Gos. Eg.	*Ox. Pap. 655*	*Gos. Thom. 37*
When Salome inquired when the things about which she asked would be known the Lord said, "When (ὅταν) on the garment (ἔνδυμα) of shame you tread."	His disciples say to him, "When will you appear to us, and when will we see you?" He says, "When (ὅταν) you take off your garments (ἐκδύσησθε) and are not ashamed [lacuna]."	His disciples said, "When will you appear to us, and when will see you?" Jesus said, "When (ⲍⲟⲧⲁⲛ) you take off your shame, and take you garments and put them under your feet, like these little children and tread on them

[94] Keeping baptism pure and undefiled (6.9; 7.1–6; 8.6) and keeping the flesh from corruption (9.3; 14.3) are probably what the preacher referred to when he said, "Now I think that I have given no mean advice concerning self-control (περὶ ἐγκρατείας)" (15.1). The contest for the crown in 7.1–6 and 20.2 might refer to sexual continence as it did in the Syrian church where keeping one's baptism pure also meant abstinence from sex (Arthur Vööbus, *Celibacy, a Requirement for Admission to Baptism in the Early Syrian Church* [Papers of the Estonian Theological Society in Exile 1; Stockholm: Estonian Theological Society in Exile, 1951] 22–23, 29).

then [you will see] the
Son of the Living (One)
and you shall not fear."

In each case Jesus is asked a question about the future
(πότε/ΠΟΤΕ), and in each case he responds with ὅταν, a reference
to shame and a verb for "taking off" or "treading" in the subjunctive mood and in the second person plural. In *Gospel of Thomas* 21a
this saying is expanded into the allegory of the children in the field.

logion 21a	logion 37
Mary said to Jesus, "Who are your disciples like?"	His disciples said, "When will you appear to us, and when will we see you?"
He said, "They are like little children who dwell in a field not theirs When the masters of the field come they will say, 'Give our field to us.' They take off their garment before them,	Jesus said, "When you take off your shame and take your garments and put them under your feet like these little children and tread on them. . . ."
to release it to them and to give back their field to them."	

In both passages the disciples are called children (Ⲛ̄ϢⲎⲢⲈ ϢⲎⲘ),
ⲌⲞⲦⲀⲚ is used to express the temporal condition, and the disciples
are told to remove their clothing (ⲔⲀⲔ ⲈⲌⲎⲨ). The allegory in
logion 21a concerns the disciples (the children) in the world (the
field), who take off their bodies (their clothing) when the rulers of
the world (the masters of the field, the archons?)[95] demand what is
theirs, the physical world and material bodies.[96]

---

[95] See Jacques-É. Ménard, *L'Évangile selon Thomas* (NHS 5: Leiden: Brill, 1975)
112–13; and Howard Clark Kee, "'Becoming a Child' in the Gospel of Thomas,"
JBL 82 (1963) 311.

[96] This interpretation of the allegory is almost universally accepted. See, e.g.,
Ménard, *L'Évangile selon Thomas*, 112–13; and Kee, "'Becoming a Child,'" 275.

B. *Becoming a Child*

This depiction of the disciples as children is consonant with the theology of the entire gospel. Rebirth for Cassianus was a return to the divine incorporeal image. For the *Gospel of Thomas*, to become a child was to return to the primordial state and to sexual perfection:[97]

> Jesus said, "Among those born of women, from Adam until John the Baptist, there is no one so superior to John the Baptist that his eyes should not be lowered (before him). Yet I have said, whichever one of you comes to be a child will be acquainted with the Kingdom and will become superior to John." (logion 46)

Concerning this passage Howard Clark Kee writes:

> Clearly this logion builds on a Q saying which occurs in slightly different forms in Matt 11:12 and Luke 16:16. In Matthew, Jesus describes an era of violence connected with the coming of the kingdom, which era extends "from the days of John the Baptist until now." In Luke, Jesus is reported as looking back to an era which began with the law and the prophets and which terminated with John. But for Thomas, the epoch under consideration began, not with John nor with the law, but with Adam; existence in this epoch is characterized by human propagation. In contrast to those in this epoch who are "born of women" are those who become as a child. The latter achieve a stage beyond—or should one say, prior to?—ordinary existence.[98]

In logion 4 we find:

> Jesus said, "The man old in days will not hesitate to ask a small child seven days old about the place of life, and he will live. For many who are first will become last [Ox. Pap. 654 adds: and the last first] and they shall become a single one."[99]

The child seven days old is living before the fall in the first week of creation, in the place of life. When his elder inquires about this

---

[97] Kee, " 'Becoming a Child,' " 307–14.

[98] Ibid., 309.

[99] For a discussion of Hippolytus's version of this logion see M. Marchovish, "Textual Criticism on the Gospel of Thomas," *JTS* 20 (1969) 60–64.

place, he becomes as he had been at first, a single one, and so shall live. This is also the meaning of logion 18:

> The disciples said to Jesus, "Tell us how our end will be." Jesus said, "Have you discovered, then, the beginning, that you look for the end? For where the beginning is, there will the end be. Blessed is he who will take his place in the beginning; he will know the end and will not experience death."

C. *The Two Are One*

It is in the context of this soteriology that one must interpret logion 22b, for it is in response to the disciples' question "Shall we then, being children, enter the Kingdom?" that Jesus says:

> When you make the two one,
> and you make
> > the inside as the outside
> > and the outside as the inside
> > and the above as the below,
> and when you make
> > the male with the female into a single one,
> > so that the male will not be male
> > and the female not female.
> When you make
> > eyes in the place of an eye,
> > and a hand in the place of a hand,
> > and a foot in the place of a foot—
> > > an image in the place of an image—
> then you shall enter the Kingdom.

When one compares this passage with others in the *Gospel of Thomas* it becomes clear that, like becoming a child, the two becoming one is a return to the primordial androgyne, much as it was for Cassianus and the *Exegesis on the Soul.*

> On the day when you were one you became two. But when you become two, what will you do? (logion 11)
>
> When you make the two one, you will become the sons of man. (logion 106)
>
> Blessed are the solitary [those who have become one] and elect, for you will find the Kingdom. For you are from it, and to it you will return. (logion 49)

The other alterations of the Dominical Saying in the *Gospel of Thomas* also speak of the believer's return to primordial oneness. For example, the author expands the phrase "the outside as the inside" (see *2 Clement*) into "the inside as the outside, and the outside as the inside, and the above as the below." The apostle Peter provides a context for understanding this enigmatic passage in his final speech in the *Acts of Peter*. Hanging upside down on a cross, Peter says:

> You must know the mystery of all nature and the beginning of all things, how it came about. For the first man, whose likeness I bear in my appearance, in falling head downwards displayed a manner of birth that was not once—for it was dead, without motion. He, being drawn down—he who also cast his first beginning down to the earth—established the whole of the cosmic system as an image of his creation (or vocation). Upside down as he was, he showed what is on the right hand as on the left, and those of the left as on the right, and changed the signs of all their nature so as to consider fair those things which were not beautiful and those things which were really evil to be good. Concerning this the Lord says in a mystery: *Unless you make what is on the right hand as what is on the left and above as what is below and what is behind as what is before—you will not have knowledge of the Kingdom.*" This thought then I have declared to you; and the form in which you now see me hanging is the representation of the man who first came to birth. You then, my beloved, both those how hear me now and those that shall hear in time, must leave your former error and turn back again." (emphasis added) [100]

In a provocative phenomenological discussion of this text, Jonathan Z. Smith shows how widespread this idea was that divine perspective is the reverse of the human, [101] and this reversal obviously is present also in the *Gospel of Thomas.*

Likewise, immediately following the Dominical Saying Jesus tells his disciples to exchange their present image with its mortal limbs for the primordial, immaterial image of God. [102]

---

[100] *Acts of Peter* 38. By comparing it with the original, I have slightly altered the translation of G. C. Stead in *NTApoc* 2. 319–20.

[101] Smith, "Birth Upside Down or Right Side Up?" *HR* 9 (1970) 281–303.

[102] The structure of the logion shows that this is an addition: observe the repetition of the phrase, "When you make."

When you make
eyes in the place of an eye,
and a hand in the place of a hand,
and a foot in the place of a foot—
an image in the place of an image. . . .

In the *Letter of Peter to Philip*, the demiurge arrogantly imitated God in wanting "to make an image in the place of an [image] and a form in the place of a form."[103] Apparently in *Gospel of Thomas* 22 the disciples are told to undo the demiurge's substitution of a material image for the primordial immaterial one.

But to understand more clearly what the evangelist meant by image (ⲍⲓⲕⲱⲛ) here, we must compare logia 84 and 85.

Jesus said, "When you see your likeness, you rejoice. But when you see your images (ⲁⲛⲉⲧⲛ̄ⲍⲓⲕⲱⲛ) which came into being before you, and which neither die nor become manifest, how much you will have to bear!"

Jesus said, "Adam came into being from a great power and a great wealth, but he did not become worthy of you. For had he been worthy, 'he would' not 'have experienced' death."

These logia interpret Gen 1:26-27, making a distinction between the "likeness" and the "image." The disciples can see their likeness, but their pre-existent image is not yet visible to them. Because he died, Adam apparently participated only in God's likeness. But the disciples, because of their eternal images, will not die. In logion 22 the distinction is not between the likeness and the image, but between two kinds of images. Nevertheless, the idea is the same: the disciples someday will trade their present image with its mortal limbs for the image according to which God created the first human.

As we have seen, each addition to the Dominical Saying in the *Gospel of Thomas* refers to the disciples' return to the perfection of paradise: they must "become like children," make "the male with the female into a single one," and replace their present image for the primordial one.

---

[103] (NHC 8, 2) 136.5–10.

The Original Meaning of the Dominical Saying

For both Clement of Alexandria and the preacher of *2 Clement* the physical creation was good, created by divine design. Therefore, for the former "the garment of shame" could not mean the body, and for the latter "the two are one" could not mean a return to the primordial androgyne. Both moralized the saying either to encourage the believer to honesty, good works, and sexual continence (*2 Clement*), or to rational obedience to the divine Logos thereby neutralizing the passions (Clement). The Dominical Saying seems to have been used in these communities by dint of its attribution to Jesus, not by dint of its theology. Its riddle-like ambiguity made it flexible enough to be used for paraenesis even by those with a different theology.[104] By the time of Origen's *First Homily on Luke 1:1*, the *Gospel of the Egyptians* had been rejected by the Egyptian church; it seems to have been used primarily by Gnostic groups thereafter. It is unlikely that the saying would have originated in communities in which it was forced into these moral allegories and from which it disappeared so quietly.

The saying seems to have been much more at home in the religious communites with which one would identify the *Gospel of the Egyptians*, Julius Cassianus, and the *Gospel of Thomas*. These three have more in common than similar interpretations of this saying. Almost everything known about the *Gospel of the Egyptians* is similar to the *Gospel of Thomas*, and since so little is known, these similarities are as suggestive as they are striking.[105] Cassianus quoted

[104] Clement of Alexandria says the saying "speaks in enigmas or riddles" ([αἰνίττεται] *Strom.* 3.13.93).

[105] Both speak of the garment of shame, the two becoming one, and Salome. Both reject childbearing and intercourse. Both speak pejoratively of women. For both, salvation is a return to the primordial state. Both seem to be sayings collections used in Egypt. The *Gospel of Thomas* was discovered in Egypt, even though many scholars argue it originated in Syria. Eastern Syrian and Egyptian Christendom in the second century shared several characteristics uncommon elsewhere, but little is known why this was the case. Since the founding of the Egyptian church is unknown to us, it is possible that Egypt had originally been evangelized by Syrian Christians who brought their sacred books with them. See Vööbus, *Celibacy*, 30. Cf. also the saying "blessed are those who fast to the world" in *Strom.* 3.16.99, apparently cited from some noncanonical gospel, and *Gos. Thom.* 27. William R. Schoedel ("Naassene Themes in the Coptic Gospel of Thomas," *VC* 14 [1960] 230) also relates the *Gospel of Thomas* to the *Gospel of the Egyptians* in saying that both were used by Naassenes.

directly from the *Gospel of the Egyptians*,[106] and shared many theological ideas with both it and the *Gospel of Thomas*.[107] These relationships of course do not mean that all three came from the same community, but they do suggest a common theological orientation and world of discourse. All three understood "the garment of shame" to refer to the body on which the believer must tread to return to perfection. "When the two become one" in each case was the reunification of the sexes. For all three "the male with the female neither male nor female" was the continent consequence of this transformation. By abstaining from sexual relations they contributed to the destruction of "the works of the female."

2.3 The Performative Setting of the Saying

None of the citations of the Dominical Saying tells us when the saying was uttered or if the conditions demanded in the saying were realized ritually. In this final section of the chapter I shall argue that the performative setting was baptism understood as rising with Christ and as returning to primordial perfection, including the disembodied, sexless state.

Ethnologists have discovered such ceremonial alterations of sexuality in religions the world over, ancient and modern.[108] Religious rites, after all, are liminal events, transforming for a time the participant's normal condition. Often these rites suspend one's psychic and physical properties as a sexual being and express one's enhanced bisexual powers or one's exchange of sexual powers, sym-

---

[106] *Strom.* 3.13.92 and possibly also 3.6.45 and 3.9.63-64.

[107] Hippolytus says the Naassenes believed, like Cassianus, that the soul descended into the body. He also says this doctrine was derived from their secret books, among which was the *Gospel of the Egyptians* (*Haer.* 8.7.8-9). See also Cyril C. Richardson, "The Gospel of Thomas, Gnostic or Encratite?" in David Neimann and Margaret Schatkin, eds., *The Heritage of the Early Church* (OrChrA 195; Rome: Pontificium Institutum Orientalium Studiorum, 1973) 75; and Gilles Quispel, "Gnosticism and the New Testament" in James Philip Hyatt, ed., *The Bible in Modern Scholarship* (Nashville: Abingdon, 1965) 256.

[108] See esp. Ernest Crawley, *Dress, Drinks, and Drums: Further Studies of Savages and Sex* (London: Methuen, 1931) 138-58; Mircea Eliade, *Mephistopheles and the Androgyne: Studies in Religious Myth and Symbol* (New York: Sheed and Ward, 1965) 78-124; and Hermann Baumann, *Das doppelte Geschlecht. Ethnologische Studien zur Bisexualität in Ritus und Mythos* (2d ed.; Berlin: Reimer, 1980).

bolized by transvestism, cosmetics, or even distortions of genitalia.[109] Sometimes, as in the Dominical Saying, such rites express entry into the sexlessness of the soul.

These rites of sexual transformation sometimes are descendants of prehistoric associations of coitus with magic, or of sympathetic fertility rites based on assumed analogies between the plow as a phallus and the earth as a womb receiving seed, or of myths of primal androgynous giants bisected at the creation of the world and cultically reunited, or of myths of world parents—Father Heaven, Mother Earth—whose act of vivification was sympathetically stimulated by sacred sex. Whatever their prehistory, rites involving alterations of one's sex were common in the ancient world and have persisted in some societies to the present.

Of course, the mythic background to the Dominical Saying is that of the primordial, incorporeal androgyne. Evidence that baptism was the primary rite symbolizing this ontological transformation comes from Valentinian Gnosticism and the Syrian Judas Didymus Thomas tradition, circles we already have identified with the Dominical Saying.

Valentinian Gnosticism

In addition to generally recognized Valentinian sources, such as the *Gospel of Truth*, the *Gospel of Philip*, and the *Excerpta ex Theodoto*, I shall incorporate into this discussion sources whose connections with Valentinianism are more tenuous, but which nonetheless evince a compatible version of Christian Gnosticism, such as the *Treatise on Resurrection*, the *Exegesis on the Soul*, and the *Tripartite Tractate*—all from Nag Hammadi.

Like Cassianus, the Valentinians Ptolemy and Theodotus called the body a "coat of skins" given the immaterial Adam at his fall.[110] Furthermore, Valentinians too believed that before death one must

[109] Baumann, *Das doppelte Geschlecht*, 352.
[110] Ptolemy (apud Iren. *Adv. haer.* 1.1.10, and Tert. *Adv. Val.* 24.3); and Theodotus (apud Clem. Al. *Exc. Theod.* 55). See also Tert. *Res. carn.* 7; idem, *De cultu feminarum* 1.1, and Origen *Cels.* 4.40.
The notion that Adam originally had been clothed in light and only later acquired skin also appears in early Jewish midrash. Louis Ginzberg cites the evidence for this in *The Legends of the Jews* (5 vols.; Philadelphia: The Jewish Publication Society of America, 1925) 5. 97, n. 69. See also *2 Enoch* 22.8; *4 Ezra* 7.97, 125; *Apoc. Moses* 20.1–3; *Asc. Isa.* 9.10. For Christian sources see Iren. *Adv. haer.* 3.23.5; and Tert. *De pudicitia* 9.

take off the body. The *Gospel of Philip* says: "Those who say they will die first and then rise are in error. If they do not first receive the resurrection while they live, when they die they will receive nothing."[111] And again: "While we are in this world it is fitting for us to acquire the resurrection for ourselves, so that when we strip off the flesh we may be found in the rest."[112]

For many Christian Gnostics one acquired resurrection in baptism. Simon Magus, Eusebius claimed, promised that those baptized by him would "obtain a share of immortality in this life itself, no longer mortal but remaining here."[113] Of Menander, Simon's disciple, Irenaeus said: "His disciples received resurrection through baptism into him, and they can no longer die, but remain without growing old and immortal."[114] According to Hippolytus, the libertine Nicolaus "was the first to affirm that the resurrection had already come; meaning by 'resurrection' the fact that we believe in Christ and have received baptism; but he denied the resurrection of the body."[115]

The same idea appears frequently in Valentinian sources. The *Treatise on Resurrection* alludes to baptism when it says: "As the Apostle said, 'We suffered with him, and we arose with him, and we went to heaven with him.' Now if we are manifest in this world wearing him, we are that one's beams."[116] The *Tripartite Tractate* says of baptism that "those who have worn it are made into light. They are the ones whom he wore."[117] That is, they once again wear the primordial garment through baptism.

The imagery used here is no doubt related to the symbolic use of garments in early baptismal rites. The initiate removed the prebaptismal garment representing the old life, was baptized naked, and put on a new white garment representing the new life. This symbolism

---

[111] (NHC 2, 3) 73.1–4; cf. the *Treat. Res.* (NHC 1, 4) 49.13–16 where the author encourages Rheginos not "to live in conformity with his flesh . . . but flee from the divisions and the fetters, and already you have the resurrection."

[112] (NHC 2, 3) 66.16–19; cf. 85.21–86. See also Tert. *De praes. haer.* 33.

[113] *Hist. eccl.* 3.26.2.

[114] *Adv. haer.* 1.23.5 (cf. Justin *1 Apol.* 1.26.1, 4).

[115] Hippol. *De resurrectione,* frg. 1 in G. N. Bonwetsch and H. Achelis, eds., *Werke* (GCS 1; Leipzig; Hinrichs, 1897) 251. Morton Smith (*Clement of Alexandria and a Secret Gospel of Mark* [Cambridge: Harvard University Press, 1973] 261–62) identified this Nicolaus with the Nicolaus of Acts 6:5 and the Nicolaitans of Rev 2:15.

[116] (NHC 1, 4) 45.24–31.

[117] (NHC 1, 5) 129.3–5; cf. *Ep. Pet. Phil.* (NHC 8, 2) 137.6–9; *Dial. Sav.* (NHC 3, 5) 16–20; *Gos. Phil.* (NHC 2, 3) 70.5–9; Iren. *Adv. haer.* 1.21.3.

was so important that baptism could even be called simply "the garment" (τὸ ἔνδυμα).[118]

Furthermore, in Valentinian initiations one not only put on light, one also reunited the sexes. As the *Gospel of Philip* says:

> The powers do not see those who are clothed in the perfect light, and consequently are not able to detain them. One will clothe himself in this light sacramentally in the union.
>
> If the woman had not separated from the man, she would not die with the man. His separation became the beginning of death. Because of this Christ came to repair the separation which was from the beginning and again unite the two, and to give life to those who died as a result of the separation and unite them. But the woman is united to her husband in the bridal chamber. Indeed those who have united in the bridal chamber will no longer be separated. Thus Eve separated from Adam because she was never united with him in the bridal chamber.[119]

This sacrament of the bridal chamber apparently was one of several Valentinian initiatory rites, one of which was baptism. *The Tripartite Tractate* shows us how closely baptism was related to the bridal chamber.

> The baptism which we previously mentioned is called "garment of those who do not strip themselves of it," for those who will put it on and those who have received redemption wear it. . . . It is also called "bridal chamber" because of the agreement and individual state of those who know that they have known him.[120]

[118] *Tri. Trac.* (NHC 1, 5) 128.19–24; *Ps.-Cl. Hom.* 8.22; *Ps.-Cl. Recog.* 4.35; and the *Acts Barn.* 12–13.

[119] (NHC 2, 3) 70.5–22. Cf. also 68.22–26: "When Eve was still in Adam death did not exist. When she was separated from him death came into being. If he again becomes complete and attains his former self, death will be no more." See also *Gos. Thom.* 75: "It is the solitary who will enter the bridal chamber." *The Dialogue of the Savior* says: "But when you remove envy from you, then you will clothe yourselves with the light and enter into the bridal chamber" [(NHC 3, 5) 138.16–20].

[120] (NHC 1, 5) 128.19–24, 33–36. The perfection of unity pervades this curious document. See also 122.2–24; 123.3–11; and 132.16–18.

Over and over again Valentinian sources speak of the unity supplied by baptism to those divided by the fall.[121] However, the fall
referred to is not always the fall of Adam and Eve. More often than
not it is the fall of the soul into the world of matter and sense-
perception. Clement's accusation that Cassianus interpreted the Dominical
Saying platonically was prompted by Cassianus's claim that "the soul
is of divine origin and, having become female by desire, has come
down here from above to birth and corruption."[122] This idea does
appear in Plato,[123] and in the Valentinian treatise entitled *Exegesis on
the Soul.* Originally the soul was virgin and bisexual, but with her
fall into the material world, she became alienated from her heavenly
syzygy and lost her virginity.

> But when she perceives the straits she is in and weeps before
> the Father and repents, then the Father will have mercy on her
> and he will make her womb turn from the external domain and
> will turn it again inward, so that the soul will regain her proper
> character. For it is not so with a woman. For the womb of the
> body is inside the body like the other internal organs, but the
> womb of the soul is around the outside like the male genitalia,
> which are external.
>
> So when the womb of the soul, by the will of the Father, turns
> itself inward, it is baptized and is immediately cleansed of the
> external pollution which was pressed upon it, just as [garments,
> when] dirty, are put into the [water and] turned about until
> their dirt is removed and they become clean. And so the cleans-
> ing of the soul is to regain the [newness] of her former nature
> and to turn herself back again. That is her baptism.[124]

Much about this passage remains obscure,[125] but several

[121] See, e.g., Clem. Al. *Exc. Theod.* 21, 22, 36, and 64. According to Irenaeus, Marcosians baptized "into union, and redemption, and communion with the Powers"
(*Adv. haer.* 1.21.3).
[122] *Strom.* 3.13.93.
[123] E.g., in *Tim.* 42a–d the soul of the wicked is changed into a woman's nature at
the second birth and remains separated from her native star until she repents. Then
she puts off her body and returns to her "first and best state," her heavenly abode.
[124] (NHC 2, 6) 131.27–132.2.
[125] I agree with William C. Robinson: "I do not understand this figure of speech [of
turning the womb of the soul] of itself and in the present context" ("The Exegesis on
the Soul," *NovT* 12 [1970] 115). Frederick Wisse suggests that "the external position
of the womb probably symbolizes that the soul has unnaturally exposed its intimate
parts, almost to invite defilement" ("On Exegeting 'The Exegesis on the Soul,'" in

observations may safely be made which are germane to this study. First, the soul's purification is from the uncleanness of the outside, that is, the body and the material world. Second, this purification, which is like washing a garment, takes place in baptism. Third, baptism returns the soul to her previous physical condition—including bisexuality—as the following passage explains:

> But then the bridegroom, according to the Father's will, came down to her into the bridal chamber, which was prepared. And he decorated the bridal chamber.
>
> For since that marriage is not like the carnal marriage, those who are to have intercourse with one another will be satisfied with the intercourse. And as if it were a burden they leave behind them the annoyance of physical desire and they do not [separate from] each other, but this marriage [. . .], but [once] they unite [with one another], they become a single life. Wherefore the prophet said concerning the first man and the first woman, "They will become a single flesh" (Gen 2:24). For they were originally joined to one another when they were with the Father before the woman led astray the man, who is her brother. This marriage has brought them back together again and the soul has been joined to her true love, her real master.[126]

Here we find clear confirming evidence that in Valentinian circles speculation on the outside becoming inside and the return of the two sexes to their primordial unity was directly related to baptism.

Now at last it should be clear how Cassianus and other Valentinians would have understood the Dominical Saying. In baptism the initiate claims to have escaped the "garment of shame," the body, and to have reunited the sexes separated at the fall—either the separation of Eve from Adam or the separation of the female soul from her heavenly male counterpart. The two again become one. Insofar as one has transcended the body and reunited the sexes, one must avoid sexual relations, that is, "the male with the female neither male nor female."

Jacques É. Ménard, ed., *Les textes de Nag Hammadi* [NHS 7; Leiden: Brill, 1975] 73).
[126] (NHC 2, 5) 132.24–133.10. Cf. *Soph. Jes. Chr.* (BG 8502, 3) 122.6–8: "I have come here that they may be united with the Spirit and with the breath, and the two become one as from the beginning."

Early Syrian Christianity

The *Gospel of Thomas* is the product of the early Syrian church, and along with *Thomas the Contender* and the *Acts of Thomas* forms a trilogy commonly referred to as the "Didymus Judas Thomas literature."[127] In addition to this trilogy, we shall examine the *Odes of Solomon* and later Syrian fathers when they preserve local traditions. The myth of the soul's descent into the material world and ultimate return appears also in Syrian Christianity. The "Hymn of the Pearl," embedded in the *Acts of Thomas*,[128] is an allegory of a king's son, the soul, sent into Egypt, the world, to recover a pearl. Before departing, the boy takes off his splendid robe and a toga which he says was "woven to the measure of my stature."[129] This robe is his heavenly alter ego, or syzygy. To disguise himself, he dresses in the Egyptian attire, that is, in a body, and subsequently forgets his mission. A letter from his parents reminds him of the pearl and his robe. Immediately he takes the pearl, and "having stripped off the filthy garment" (ἀποδυσάμενος τὸ ῥυπαρὸν ἔνδυμα), he leaves it "in their field" and speeds to his father's kingdom. His reunion with his father is a mere adumbration when compared with his literal "reunion" with his robe.

> Indeed I had forgotten its brightness, for when I was a child and a young man I left it in my father's palaces. But immediately when I saw the garment, it became like me, as a reflection in a mirror, and I saw myself wholly in it. And I knew and saw myself because of it, because often we had been divided, although we both were from him [or: it] and again we were one in one form. Also the treasurers who had brought the garment to me I found to be two, but one form was on both: one royal sign was on them both. . . . And the image of the king of kings was entirely on it (the robe).[130]

In this version of the myth, the two that become one are not the two sexes or the female soul and her male heavenly counterpart, but the boy and his robe. Nonetheless, the underlying soteriology and

---

[127] For justification in linking these works with each other see Helmut Koester, "*Gnomai Diaphoroi*: The Origin and Nature of Diversification in the History of Early Christianity," in James M. Robinson and idem, *Trajectories Through Early Christianity* (Philadelphia: Fortress, 1971) 126–43.

[128] *Acts Thom.* 108–13.

[129] Ibid., 108.

[130] Ibid., 113.

anthropology are identical: before death (here by receiving the
heavenly revelation), the soul returns to its place of origin and is
joined to its syzygy. Both the *Gospel of Thomas* and *Thomas the Contender* command the reader to leave the body.[131]
The *Odes of Solomon* were compiled in Syria during the same
period, and here again the images of putting off the body and of putting on light (or incorruption, or the spirit, or a new body) appear in
the context of baptism.[132]

> And I was clothed with the clothing of your Spirit,
> And I took away from me my garments of skin,[133]
> Because your right hand had lifted me up,
> And you made pain pass from me. (25:8-9)

> And I rejected the folly cast upon the earth,
> And stripped it off and cast it from me.
> And the Lord renewed me with his garment,
> And possessed me by his light.
> And from above he gave me immortal rest,
> And I became like the land that blossoms
>   and rejoices. (11:10-12)

> And I put off darkness,
> And put on light.
> And even I myself acquired members.
> In them there was no sickness
>   or affliction or suffering. (21:3-4)

Like Valentinians, Syrian Christians maintained that this new condition created by the liberation of the soul from the body required an
alteration of sexuality. By examining early Syrian liturgies, Arthur
Vööbus and Robert Murray have demonstrated that asceticism was in
fact prerequisite for baptism.

[131] E.g., *Gos. Thom.* 21, 27 and *Thom. Cont.* (NHC 2,7) 145.1-17.

[132] Eric Segelberg ("The Baptismal Rite according to some of the Coptic-Gnostic
Texts of Nag-Hammadi," in F. L. Cross, ed., *International Conference on Patristic Studies* [TU 80; *StPatr* 5; Berlin: Akademie-Verlag, 1962] 118) states: "In the Odes there
are a good many references to baptismal ritual which enable us to reconstruct a good
deal of the baptismal ritual of the Odes."

[133] Cf. Jerome's *Epistle to Fabiola* 19 (as quoted by Jonathan Z. Smith, "The Garments of Shame," *HR* 5 [1966] 232-33): "And when ready for the garment of
Christ, we have taken off the coats of skins, then we shall be clothed with a garment
of linen which has nothing of death in it, but is wholly white so that, rising from baptism, we may gird our loins in truth and the entire shame of our past sins may be
covered."

With regards to the sacraments, baptism became the prerogative of the ascetic elite only. It became the sign of those who had courage to make the radical decision to turn their backs decisively upon the world and walk in conformity with new standards.[134]

Tertullian wrote of Marcion, who was influential in Syria: "The flesh is not . . . immersed in the water of the sacrament, unless it be in virginity, widowhood, or celibacy, or has purchased by divorce a title to baptism."[135] But mainstream Syrian Christianity too recognized this requirement. In Ephraem's eighth baptismal hymn from *On Epiphany* we find:

> See, (people) being baptized and becoming
> virgins and consecrated ones,
> having gone down, been baptized and put on
> that single "Only One."[136]

Asceticism is also a requirement for baptism in the *Acts of Thomas*, as Vööbus has shown:

> The relation between baptism and celibacy will be illustrated . . . in an episode with Vazan, a young man, who is also a convert of Thomas. He reveals his ripe intention to be baptized. He confesses to the Apostle that he has been compelled to marry and that he has kept his virginity during the whole marital period. All this sounds as though he feels that he is entitled to receive baptism because he has already shown himself capable of keeping his virginity, which is the condition laid down for the reception of this sacrament.[137]

---

[134] Vööbus, *The History of Asceticism in the Syrian Orient: A Contribution to the History of Culture in the Near East* (Papers of the Estonian Theological Society in Exile 1; Stockholm: Estonian Theological Society in Exile, 1951) 90. See also Robert Murray, "The Exhortation to Candidates for Ascetical Vows at Baptism in the Ancient Syriac Church," *NTS* 21 (1974) 59–80; and Karl Müller, "Die Forderung der Ehelosigkeit für alle Getauften in der alten Kirche," in idem, *Aus der akademischen Arbeit* (Tübingen: Mohr-Siebeck, 1930) 63–79.

[135] *Adv. Marc.* 1.29. For evidence of Marcion's influence in Syria see Walter Bauer, *Orthodoxy and Heresy in Earliest Christianity* (Philadelphia: Fortress, 1971) 21–38.

[136] As quoted in Murray, "Exhortation," 64. The text appears in *Des heiligen Ephraem des Syrers Hymnen de Nativitate (Epiphania)* (ed. Edmund Beck; CSCO 186, Syr. 82; Louvain: Secrétariat du Corpus SCO, 1959) 173.

[137] Vööbus, *Celibacy*, 27–28.

Similarly, Siphor promises Thomas, "I and my wife and my daughter will live henceforth in holiness and [sexual][138] purity, and in one mind. I beg you that we may receive the seal from you."[139]

One episode in the *Acts of Thomas* in particular demands our attention. In sections 12-14 Thomas tells a couple in a bridal chamber:

> But if you obey and keep your souls pure unto God, you shall have living children whom these hurts do not touch, and shall be without care, leading an undisturbed life without grief or anxiety, waiting to receive that incorruptible and true marriage . . . and in it you shall be groomsmen entering into that bridal chamber which is full of immortality and light.[140]

The couple refrain from consummating the wedding and tell her father in unison:

> Truly, father, we are greatly in love, and have been persuaded by the Lord . . . we have been rescued from temporary intercourse and corruption. Wherefore we have been yoked together in a firm and true marriage and *the garment of shame* (τὸ ἔνδυμα τῆς αἰσχύνης) has been taken from us. (emphasis added) [141]

This text surely is a conscious interpretation of the Dominical Saying. To my knowledge this is the only place outside of direct references to the Dominical Saying in which τὸ ἔνδυμα τῆς αἰσχύνης appears in early Christian literature. But the claim for a conscious dependence is not merely lexical. Textual authorities for this section may be divided into two traditions.[142] "The garment of shame"

---

[138] For a defense of "purity" here meaning sexual abstinence, see Murray, "Exhortation," 74.

[139] *Acts Thom.* 131.

[140] Ibid., 12. So also, after her baptism, Mygdonia rejects her husband's advances and contrasts her marriage to him to that to Christ. Here, as in Valentinianism, baptism is called the bridal chamber:

> Thou hast seen that marriage which passed away [and remains here (on earth)], but this marriage abides forever. . . . That bridal chamber is taken down, but this remains forever. . . . Thou art a bridegroom who passes away and is destroyed, but Jesus is a true bridegroom, abiding immortal forever. (124)

[141] Ibid., 14.

[142] It is unnecessary for our purposes to solve the complex relations between these textual traditions and their many variants. My preference would be to take the shorter version as the earlier, since by giving both the bride and the groom their own

appears only in the shorter tradition, [143] and it is also only in the shorter text that "the two become one." When the king, her father, enters the nuptial chamber, he sees the couple sitting apart from each other "unyoked" (διαζευγμένοι) which can also mean "divorced." In response to his questioning why they seem so cold to each other, they reply in unison that they have been "yoked together" in a true marriage. In the worldly bridal chamber the pair are separated, unyoked, but in the true bridal chamber, baptism, they are yoked together. They have removed the garment of shame and the two have become one; therefore, no longer can they respond to each other as male and female.

Therefore, in both Valentinianism, from which Cassianus came, and in Syrian Christendom, from which the *Gospel of Thomas* came, the Dominical Saying was interpreted similarly. At baptism the initiate symbolized his or her flight from the body by removing the prebaptismal "garment of shame," and symbolized making the outside like the inside, putting on light or being reunited with the heavenly self, by putting on the postbaptismal garment. One demonstrated this new transcendent condition by remaining sexually ascetic. When the male was with the female they could no longer respond as male or female.

Treading on the Garment of Shame

According to the Dominical Saying, one must not only remove the "garment of shame," one must also tread on it. This may be a figure unrelated to actual baptismal practice, but there is evidence that sometimes the prebaptismal garment was in fact trampled.

Much of the evidence for this practice has been collected by Jonathan Z. Smith in an imaginative article entitled "The Garments of Shame," where he suggests that the *Sitz im Leben* of the command to take off and tread on one's clothing in *Gospel of Thomas* 37

---

speeches, the longer tradition was able to insert a long prayer of thanksgiving. I can detect no reason for the shorter to have omitted the prayer. Actually, the case for the dependence on the Dominical Saying is as strong or stronger if the opposite were the case: the alterations of the longer text by the shorter would then show a conscious reworking toward the saying by altering τὸ ἔσοπτρον to τὸ ἔνδυμα, by inserting the word play on διαζεύγνυμι and συζεύγνυμι, and by having the couple speak in unison.

[143] The longer reads τὸ ἔσοπτρον τῆς αἰσχύνης or τὸ ἔργον τῆς αἰσχύνης.

was this baptismal rite. [144] His sources are Augustine and Theodore of Mopsuestia, both of whom lived in the late fourth and early fifth centuries. Even though one must be cautious in using such late sources, it is certain that Augustine and Theodore did indeed refer to practices common in earlier Gnostic circles.

Theodore says the baptismal service was preceded by an exorcism in which the catechumen removed a garment of sackcloth and stood on it barefooted, "so that from the fact your feet are pricked and stung by the roughness of the cloth you may remember your old sins and show penitence and repentance of the sins of your fathers." [145] Augustine tells of exorcisms in which the catechumen stood not on sackcloth but on a goatskin: "so sin is trampled underfoot as is the goatskin." [146] It is unlikely that the skin or sackcloth originally represented sin. More likely it represented the body which one treated with contempt by trampling it prior to baptism. I suggest this was the original significance of the rite. Theodore and Augustine later simply moralized the symbol and made it represent repentance and disdain for one's past sins.

This suggestion is confirmed by evidence already in the second century that trampling on the powers of darkness, whose domain of course included the body, was related to baptism. The Valentinian Theodotus said: "The one baptized unto God has gone to God and has received 'power to walk upon scorpions and snakes,' the evil powers." [147] The Nag Hammadi fragment entitled *On the Anointing*, commonly identified as Valentinian, has an almost identical reference, although here it is in the context of the postbaptismal unction: "It is fitting for [thee at this time] to send thy Son [Jesu]s Christ and anoint us so that we might be able to trample upon the [snakes] and [the heads] of the scorpions and [all] the power of the Devil." [148]

Trampling on the powers in baptism also appears in *The Hypostasis of the Archons*. Responding to the question "How long before the kingdom comes?" the revealer says:

[144] Smith, "Garments of Shame," *HR* 5 (1966) 217–38.
[145] Alphonse Mingana, *Commentary of Theodore of Mopsuestia on the Lord's Prayer and on the Sacraments of Baptism and the Eucharist* (Woodbrooke Studies 6; Cambridge: Heffer and Sons, 1933) 31–32.
[146] Sermon 216, 10, *PL* XXXVIII, 1082; cf. Hildefonse of Toledo (7th century), *De cognitione baptismi* 14, *PL* XCVI, 116–17.
[147] Clem. Al. *Exc. Theod.* 76 (quoting Luke 10:19). See also *Strom.* 4.6, where Clement himself seems to hold a similar notion.
[148] (NHC 11, 2a) 40.11–17.

Then he will teach them about everything: And he will anoint them with the unction of Life eternal, given him from the undominated generation.

Then they will be freed of blind thought: And they will trample under foot Death, which is of the Authorities: And they will ascend into the limitless Light, where this Sown Element belongs. [149]

Inasmuch as baptism was frequently related to the unction and to the rising to "infinite light," this passage may well be another witness to treading on the powers in baptism. In *Sophia Jesu Christi* we find: "I have given you power over all things as sons of light, so that you might tread upon their power with [your] feet."[150]

In Syria too there is evidence that in baptism one trod on the prebaptismal garment. For example, in a baptismal homily of Narsai (399-503 CE?) we find: "They that were clothed with passions have put on hidden power from the water; and they have begun to defy the Foe, that they may trample on his power."[151]

Therefore, it is not pressing the evidence unduly to suggest that the rite of treading on the prebaptismal garment mentioned by Theodore and Augustine originated in circles for whom baptism entitled one to tread on the body, the product and prey of evil powers, which the skin or garment symbolized. References to treading appear in baptismal contexts already in the second century and in those very groups where baptism symbolized the initiate's transcending the body and thereby escaping the tether of the dark powers.

Conclusion

The Dominical Saying is an early Christian baptismal saying dramatizing the initiate's putting off the body, putting on light, and returning to sexual oneness. In some communities, the prebaptismal garment was trampled as a symbol of disdain for the body and its governing powers. One result of this putative return was celibacy.

[149] (NHC 2, 4) 97.2–9.
[150] (NHC 3, 4) 119.4–8.
[151] Richard Hugh Connolly, *The Liturgical Homilies of Narsai* (Reprint, Texts and Studies: Contributions to Biblical and Patristic Literature 8, 19 [Nendeln: Kraus Reprint, 1967] 54).

This baptismal soteriology obviously was current in Egypt and Syria early in the second century, and was dominant in Valentinian Gnostic and Syrian "Thomas" circles. But, as we shall now see, it was already present in Pauline communities by the time Paul wrote Galatians.

3

RITUAL, SEX, AND VEILS AT CORINTH

The identity of Paul's opponents in Corinth has proved one of the most controversial and slippery issues in the interpretation of the New Testament. John J. Gunther has isolated thirteen different hypotheses, including Judaizers, Alexandrian pneumatic Jews, ascetic Gnostics, and libertine Gnostics.[1] From this confusion, however, something of a consensus has recently emerged concerning the religious mentality that birthed Corinthian theology on the one hand and the descendents of that theology on the other. The mother was Hellenistic Judaism; the descendents, Christian Gnosticism.

Richard A. Horsley has accumulated an impressive number of parallels between Philo and the theology Paul confronted at Corinth, though he surely overstates his case by suggesting the Corinthians were Philo-like mystics behind a thin Christian veneer.[2] Acts 18:24-25 may explain how this theology got to Corinth.

---

[1] Gunther, *St. Paul's Opponents and Their Background: A Study of Apocalyptic and Sectarian Teachings* (NovTSup 35; Leiden: Brill, 1973) 1.

[2] Horsley, "Paul and the *Pneumatikoi*: First Corinthians Investigated in Terms of the Conflict between Two Different Religious Mentalities" (Ph.D. diss., Harvard University, 1970). In addition to this original research, Horsley has published a number of articles: "Pneumatikos vs Psychikos: Distinctions of Spiritual Status Among the Corinthians," *HTR* 69 (1976) 269-88; "Wisdom of Word and Words of Wisdom in Corinth," *CBQ* 39 (1977) 224-39; "The Background of the Confessional Formula in 1 Kor 8:6," *ZNW* 69 (1978) 130-35; "Spiritual Marriage with Sophia," *VC* 33 (1979) 30-54; and "Gnosis in Corinth: 1 Cor 8:1-6," *NTS* 27 (1980) 32-51.

> Now a Jew named Apollos, a native of Alexandria, came to
> Ephesus. He was an eloquent man, well versed in the scrip-
> tures. He had been instructed in the way of the Lord; and being
> fervent in spirit, he spoke and taught accurately the things con-
> cerning Jesus, though he knew only the baptism of John.

Apollos, an Alexandrian Jew educated in biblical exegesis, arrived
in Corinth sometime during the years 50 and 51. The author of Acts
would have us believe that Apollos and Paul were congenial col-
leagues in Corinth, but several scholars have shown rather convinc-
ingly that they were in fact antagonists.[3] The antagonism was due in
large part to fundamentally competing religious mentalities: Apollos's
Philo-like mysticism and Paul's apocalypticism.

On the other hand, aspects of Corinthian theology also appear in
later Christian Gnosticism, as illustrated by the remarkable number
of parallels unearthed by Walther Schmithals.[4] Many of these must
be granted, even though he obscures the discussion by referring to
the Corinthians themselves as Gnostics. Absent from 1 Corinthians
are traces of the "Gnostic myth"; present in abundance are the
vocabulary, Genesis speculations, sacramentalism, and anthropology
of later Christian Gnostics. Furthermore, James M. Robinson has
suggested that the Corinthians transmitted Jesus traditions similar to
those which ultimately found their way into the *Gospel of Thomas*
and the Valentinian *Gospel of Philip*.[5] He links these traditions explicitly to Gnostic baptismal resurrections.

Robert McL. Wilson prudently warns that one must not confuse
gnosis, a popular and protean religious mentality, with Gnosticism,
which is best reserved for referring more exactly to the classical
Gnostic systems of the second and subsequent centuries.[6] Corinthian
theology falls into the first category, not the second.

> I Corinthians shows "into how congenial a soil the seeds of
> Gnosticism were about to fall." We may suspect today that
> some of the seeds had already been sown, that some of them
> indeed had even begun to germinate. What is certain is that in

---

[3] See Helmut Koester, "*Gnomai Diaphoroi*: The Origin and Nature of
Diversification in the History of Early Christianity," in James M. Robinson and idem,
Trajectories Through Early Christianity (Philadelphia: Fortress, 1971) 149; Birger A.
Pearson, *The Pneumatikos-Psychikos Terminology* (SBLDS 12; Missoula: Scholars Press,
1973) 18; and Horsley, "Paul and the *Pneumatikoi*" 164–65.

[4] Schmithals, *Gnosticism in Corinth.*

[5] Robinson, "Kerygma and History in the New Testament," in *Trajectories*, 30–46.

[6] Wilson, "How Gnostic Were the Corinthians?" *NTS* 19 (1972).

the New Testament period the field is still far from being ripe
for the harvest. Gnosis in the broader sense is not yet Gnosticism, and to interpret New Testament texts which *may* reflect
Gnosis in terms of later Gnosticism is to run the risk of distort-
ing the whole picture.[7]

It would therefore appear that the theology of the "pneumatics,"
or the "spiritual," at Corinth may be considered a variation of
gnosis, a bend in a stream of tradition flowing from Philo to later
Christian Gnosticism. It is not possible here to chart the course of
that stream in detail. For our purposes it is sufficient to show that
the anthropology, sacramentology, and Genesis speculations present
in the Dominical Saying had flowed into Corinth by the time Paul
wrote Galatians.

3.1 Baptism and the Garment of Shame

The "pneumatics" at Corinth believed they had already cast off the
garment of flesh. As James Robinson puts it:

> When Paul criticizes "some of you" for asserting that "there is
> no resurrection of the dead" (1 Cor 15:12), one . . . assumes he
> is alluding to a position that is not to be taken as the enlighted
> rationalism of the Greek philosophical mind but rather as the
> turgid fanaticism of those who have already risen and are living
> it up in glory. For although the word *already* is lacking in 15:12,
> it is present with all its presumptions and potentially heretical
> overtones in Paul's description of his opponents in 1 Cor 4:8:
> "Already you have feasted to the full; already you have reached
> wealth; without us you have taken over the reign."[8]

All things were lawful for them (6:12; 10:23), and all things were
theirs (3:21). They were the wise (1:21–2:16; 3:18–23; 8:1), the
perfect (2:6), the spiritual (2:15; 3:1; 12:1; 14:37). Their imperish-
able souls had put off the body; this immortal had put off the mortal.
Paul argued precisely the opposite:

> This perishable nature must *put on* (ἐνδύσασθαι) the imperish-
> able, and this mortal nature must *put on* (ἐνδύσασθαι) immor-
> tality. When the perishable *puts on* (ἐνδύσηται) the imperish-
> able, and the moral *puts on* (ἐνδύσηται) immortality, *then* shall

---

[7] Ibid., 71.
[8] Robinson, "Kerygma and History," 33–34.

come to pass the saying that is written: "Death is swallowed in victory. O Death, where is thy victory? O Death, where is thy sting?" (15:53-54)

For Paul, incorruptibility and immortality are eschatological possessions, not present states of existence. Whether at the Parousia, as here, or at death, as in 2 Cor 5:1-4, one does not put off the body; the body puts on immortality.[9]

Furthermore, when Paul argued for the eschatological resurrection of the body against his opponents' putative release of the soul, he provided his own interpretation of the first and second Adams. For Philo, Valentinians, and Syrian Christians, the first Adam was the heavenly and the second the earthly. But for Paul it was the *second* Adam, Christ, who was the heavenly:

> Thus it is written, "The first Adam became a living soul"; the last Adam became a life-giving spirit. But it is not the pneumatic which is first but the psychic, and then the pneumatic. The first human was from the earth, clay-like; the second human is from heaven. As was the clay-like human, so are the clay-like; and as is the heavenly human, so are the heavenly. Just as we have worn the image of the clay-like, we shall also wear the image of the heavenly. (15:45-49)

Even though Paul says believers "no longer wear the image" of the first Adam, he refuses to say they now wear the image of the heavenly: "We *shall* wear the image of the heavenly." Only at the Parousia will the Corinthians "be made alive":

> For as in Adam all died,
> in Christ *will* all be made alive,
> *but each in its own order*:
> Christ the first fruits,

---

[9] Horsley rightly comments: "The notion of this mortal nature putting on immortality is clearly opposed to the whole structure of understanding in which the immortal soul strips off the mortal body as the soteriological solution to having put on the body. Paul uses the Corinthians' own terminology in the contrasts mortal-immortal, corruptible-incorruptible. Yet in re-setting these terms into his own eschatological pattern of thinking he says something quite different from what the pneumatikoi were thinking. . . . Paul shifts the focus decisively from the exclusive spiritual existence of the true self available only to the religious elite to the (still future) eschatological transformation of existence which will take place in the resurrection" ("Paul and the *Pneumatikoi*," 367).

> *then* those who belong to Christ *at his parousia*,
> *then* comes the end,
>   when he will deliver the kingdom
>   to God the Father,
>   when he will destroy every kingdom
>   and every authority and power. . . .
>   The *last* enemy to be conquered is death. (15:22–26)

This apocalyptic periodization polemicizes against those who claimed they had already conquered death. The basis for this claim may well have been their understanding of baptism.

In 1 Cor 10:1–12, Paul says that even though all the Hebrews were baptized into Moses and all ate pneumatic food and drank pneumatic drink, God smote the majority of them in the desert because of disobedience. This allegory counters the Corinthians' presumption of ethical perfection by virtue of the sacraments. Hence Paul's warning in 10:12: "Let him who thinks he stands" by virtue of the sacraments "take heed lest he fall."

Of course, identifying baptism with moral perfection does not *eo ipso* require one to conclude that the Corinthians thought baptism delivered them from the body. Evidence of this comes from 1 Cor 15:29, "one of the most hotly disputed passages in the epistle."[10] It is my view that behind this passage is a crisis caused by the fact that some at Corinth had died unbaptized. Inasmuch as baptism secured the release of the soul, the Corinthians considered the souls of these dead to be trapped in corpses. By being baptized for the dead, some Corinthians hoped to secure the release of these souls. Whether or not this interpretation is correct—and it certainly may be debated— baptism in Corinth seems to have been connected with moral and ontological perfection.

3.2 Sex and the Sayings of Jesus

If the Corinthians thought they had already been liberated from the material world and returned to the primordial state, we might expect alterations in their attitudes toward sexuality. This was in fact the case. One member had an affair with his stepmother, and some in the community boasted about it (5:2). Others patronized prostitutes on the pretext that "all things are permissible" (6:12).

---

[10] Hans Conzelmann, *1 Corinthians* (Hermeneia; Philadelphia: Fortress, 1969) 275.

Most of the Corinthians, however, were not libertine; in fact, some in Corinth claimed: "It is good for a man not to touch a woman" (7:2). This radical polarization in Corinthian sexual mores might best be explained by the conviction, shared by both groups, that they had transcended the material world, including sexuality. This transcendence for some meant freedom to perform any sexual act, and for others it meant rejection of all sexual acts. It is difficult to postulate another solution for the wide behavioral distance between these two factions of the same community.[11]

Of course, the currency in Corinth of the imagery and theological anthropology of the Dominical Saying does not prove the saying itself was known there. However, in 1 Corinthians, in the context of his treatment of sexuality, Paul shows an interest in sayings of Jesus unparalleled in the rest of his letters: "To the married I give charge, not I but the Lord . . ." (7:10);[12] "To the rest I say, not the Lord . . . " (7:12); and "Now concerning the virgins, I have no command from the Lord . . ."(7:25).

David L. Balch suggests that Paul was obligated to discuss the issue of celibacy with reference to sayings of Jesus because it was precisely these sayings that motivated and justified Corinthian asceticism.[13] The Synoptic tradition did indeed include sayings of Jesus congenial to asceticism:

> If anyone comes to me and does not hate his own father and mother *and wife* and children and brothers and sisters . . . he cannot be my disciple. (Luke 14:26)

> There is no one who has left house *or wife* or brothers or parents or children for the sake of the kingdom of God who will not receive manifold more in this time, and in the age to come eternal life. (Luke 18:29–30)

> As it was in the day of Noah, so will it be in the days of the Son of man. They ate, they drank, they married, they were given in marriage, until the day when Noah entered the ark, and the flood came and destroyed them all. (Luke 17:26–27)

---

[11] See Victor Paul Furnish, *The Moral Teaching of Paul* (Nashville: Abingdon, 1979) 97. Note, however, John C. Hurd, Jr., *The Origin of I Corinthians* (London: SPCK; New York: Seabury, 1965) 164.

[12] This is the only place in chap. 7 in which Paul claims the Lord's authority. The tradition referred to probably is Jesus' prohibition of divorce recorded in Mark 10:1–10 (// Matt 19:3–9).

[13] "Background of I Cor. VII: Sayings of the Lord in Q; Moses as a ΘΕΙΟΣ ΑΝΗΡ in II Cor. III," *NTS* 18 (1972) 351–64.

In Luke's version of the Parable of the Great Supper (14:20), one of the guests invited to the heavenly banquet disqualifies himself on the grounds that he has married a wife. Although much of Balch's theory is speculative, he anchors it in an astute lexical observation.

> The interpretation and translation of the verbs γαμέω and γαμίζω in I Cor. 7:36 and 38 has always been hotly disputed. Kugelmann calls the latter verb "the key word on which the exegesis of this entire passage depends." It is, then, extremely striking that these two verbs occur together in Q and that they appear together in the very passages in Luke which I suggest were being discussed in Corinth (Luke 20:35 = Matt 22:30 = Mark 12:25 and Luke 17:27 = Matt 24:38). To this must be added the fact that the rare form γαμίζω (causative?) does not appear anywhere else in the NT (or OT) and is found only in Apollonius Dyscolus (*Syntax* 280. 11) [second century CE] in extra-biblical Greek. The phrase "marrying and giving in marriage" . . . was, therefore, almost certainly a catch-phrase . . . which Paul is forced to discuss in I Cor 7 (esp. verses 36 – 38).[14]

One might press Balch's observation one step further. The verbs γαμέω and γαμίζω appear together in only two gospel sayings: in Luke 17:26 – 27 (= Matt 24:37 – 39), quoted above, and in Mark 12:18 – 27 where Sadduccees ask Jesus concerning a woman married seven times: "In the resurrection whose wife will she be?" Jesus answers, "When they are raised from the dead they neither marry nor are given in marriage, for they are like angels in heaven" (12:25). Had the Corinthians known this saying, as the use of γαμίζω in 1 Cor 7:38 might suggest, they might have refused marriage on the ground that they already had been raised. This is precisely how the passage was interpreted by Cassianus: his followers "neither marry nor are given in marriage" because "they already have attained the state of resurrection."[15]

---

[14] Ibid., 357.
[15] Clem. Al. *Strom.* 3.6.47 – 48. Luke's version of Mark 12:18 – 27 likewise makes it an appeal for celibacy. Here marriage is rejected not just in the resurrection, but already now for "those worthy of the resurrection of the dead . . . for they cannot die, for they are like angels, and being sons of God they are sons of the resurrection" (Luke 20:34 – 35).

We shall never know for certain if the Dominical Saying was among those Jesus traditions used at Corinth to support celibacy. Nonetheless, as we now shall see, the Corinthians did employ the Genesis speculation presupposed by the saying to justify women's removing their head coverings in prayer and prophecy.

3.3 Women and Veils of Authority

The Problem

Without question, 1 Cor 11:2–16 is "one of the most obscure passages in the Pauline letters,"[16] a linguistic labyrinth rivaling Daedalus's and befuddling a host of would-be Theseuses. Every turn in this maze forces the intruder to choose from among several paths.

> I praise you for remembering me in all respects and for maintaining the traditions as I passed them on to you. (vs 2)

Does this verse pertain to what precedes or to what follows? If to the rebuke that follows, how should one understand this expression of praise? Was the problem created by the Corinthians' faithfulness to Paul's own teachings?[17] Or is it a *captatio benevolentiae*, a literary stratagem for ingratiating oneself to readers before scolding them?[18]

> But I wish you to know that Christ is the head (κεφαλή) of every man, and the man the head (κεφαλή) of a woman, and God head (κεφαλή) of Christ. (vs 3)

---

[16] Wayne A. Meeks, *The Writings of St. Paul* (New York: Norton, 1972) 38. For a partial account of the research on this passage in English publications, see Linda Mercadante, *From Hierarchy to Equality: A Comparison of Past and Present Interpretations of 1 Cor 11:2–16 in Relation to the Changing Status of Women in Society* (Vancouver: G-M-H Books, 1978).

[17] E.g., Schüssler Fiorenza (*In Memory of Her*, 228–29) claims the tradition was Paul's own teaching concerning liberation and freedom. See also Evans, *Woman in the Bible*, 83–84.

[18] Meeks, "Image of the Androgyne," 202; and Conzelmann, *1 Corinthians*, 182. Marco Adinolfi ("Il velo della donna e la rilettura paolina di 1 Cor. 11, 2–16," *RevistB* 23 [1975] 166) argues that the tradition referred to in vs 2 is the Palestinian custom of veiling women, a custom sometimes violated at Corinth.

Does κεφαλή here mean source as in a sequence of generation,[19] or superior as in a ranking of ontological value,[20] or both?[21]

> Every man who prays or prophesies having something on his head (κατὰ κεφαλῆς ἔχων) shames his head; and every woman who prays or prophecies with her head uncovered (ἀκατακαλύπτῳ) shames her head, for she is no different from a woman who has had her head shaved. For if a woman is not covered, let her be shorn. And if it is shameful for a woman to be shorn or shaved, let her be covered. (vss 4–6)

Is Paul debunking the behavior of both men and women or just of the women?[22] What is meant by "having something on his head" (κατὰ κεφαλῆς ἔχων)? Does it refer to long hair or to head

[19] Leenhardt, "La place de la femme," 17–20; Hick, *Stellung des hl. Paulus,* 121–24; Kähler, *Frau,* 52–53; Morna Hooker, "Authority on Her Head: An Examination of 1 Cor. XI. 10," *NTS* (1964) 410–11; C. K. Barrett, *The First Epistle of St Paul to the Corinthians* (New York: Harper & Row, 1968) 248; F. F. Bruce, *1 and 2 Corinthians* (New Century Bible; Greenwood, SC: Attic, 1978) 103; Scroggs, "Paul and the Eschatological Woman," 298–301; and idem, "Paul and the Eschatological Woman: Revisited," *JAAR* 42 (1974) 534; Furnish, *Moral Teaching of Paul,* 98–99; Adinolfi, "La velo della dona," 166–69; and Jerome Murphy-O'Connor, "Sex and Logic in 1 Corinthians 11:2–16," *CBQ* 42 (1980) 491–93.

[20] Archibald Robertson and Alfred Plummer, *A Critical and Exegetical Commentary on the First Epistle of St Paul to the Corinthians* (2d ed.; ICC; Edinburgh: T. & T. Clark, 1914) 229; F. W. Grosheide, *Commentary on the First Epistle to the Corinthians* (NICNT; Grand Rapids: Eerdmans, 1953) 249–50; Jervell, *Imago Dei,* 301–3; Abel Isaksson, *Marriage and Ministry in the New Temple: A Study with Special Reference to Matt 19.3–12 and 1 Cor. 11.3–16* (Lund: Gleerup; Copenhagen: Munksgaard, 1965) 164, n. 2; and Hurley, *Man and Woman,* 163–68.

[21] Johannes Weiss, *Der erste Korintherbrief* (MeyerK 5; 9th ed.; Göttingen: Vandenhoeck & Ruprecht, 1910) 269–70; Tischleder, *Wesen und Stellung,* 143–46; Stephen Bedale, "The Meaning of *kephale* in the Pauline Epistles," *JTS* n.s. 5 (1954) 211–15; Leon Morris, *The First Epistle of Paul to the Corinthians* (Tyndale New Testament Commentaries; London: Tyndale, 1958) 151–52; Jean Héring, *The First Epistle of St. Paul to the Corinthians* (London: Epworth, 1962) 102; Meeks, "Image of the Androgyne," 200; Conzelmann, *1 Corinthians,* 183; John P. Meier, "On the Veiling of Hermeneutics (1 Cor. 11:2–16)," *CBQ* 40 (1978) 217–18; Susan T. Foh, *Women and the Word of God: A Response to Biblical Feminism* (Philadelphia: Presbyterian and Reformed Publishing Co., 1979) 101–2; and Clark, *Man and Woman in Christ,* 177–80.

[22] Only a few scholars have thought the men altered their heads as well; e.g., Murphy-O'Connor, "Sex and Logic," 483–84; Richard and Catherine Kroeger, "An Inquiry into Evidence of Maenadism in the Corinthian Congregation," in Paul J. Achtemeier, ed., *SBL 1978 Seminar Papers* (Missoula: Scholars Press, 1978) 2. 331–33.

coverings?[23] What is meant by "with her head uncovered" (ἀκατακαλύπτῳ)? Again, does it refer to short hair, long hair unbound, or to the removal of veils? How is Paul using the word κεφαλή here? Is the head the man "shames" his own anatomical head, or Christ, his metaphorical "head" as in vs 3? Likewise, is the head the woman "shames" her anatomical or her metaphorical "head," that is, the man?[24] How did women of the time adorn their heads? Did women of all ages wear veils, or just older and married women? Did they wear them only in public or also at home? Were the conventions followed by Jewish women the same as those fol-

---

[23] Most interpreters have understood it to refer to head coverings. Those who think it refers to hair styles include: Isaksson, *Marriage and Ministry*, 166–85; William J. Martin, "I Corinthians 11:2–16: An Interpretation," in W. W. Gasque and R. P. Martyn, eds., *Apostolic History and the Gospel* (Grand Rapids: Eerdmans, 1970) 233–34; James B. Hurley, "Did Paul Require Veils or the Silence of Women? A Consideration of I Cor 11,2–16 and I Cor 14,33b–36," *WTJ* 35 (1973) 190–220; and idem, *Man and Woman*, 168–71; Stephen A. Reynolds, "Colloquium," *WTJ* 36 (1973) 90–91; Jerome Murphy-O'Connor, "The Non-Pauline Character of 1 Corinthians 11:2–16?" *JBL* 95 (1976) 620–21; and idem, "Sex and Logic," 482–500; Robert Banks, "Paul and Women's Liberation," *Interchange* 18 (1976) 81–104; Evans, *Woman in the Bible*, 87–88; Schüssler Fiorenza, *In Memory of Her*, 227–29; and Alan Padgett, "Paul on Women in the Church: The Contradictions of Coiffure in 1 Corinthians 11:2–16," *JSNT* 20 (1984) 70. I reject as preposterous Martin's suggestion ("1 Corinthians 11:2–16," 234–41) that 1 Cor 11:2–16 merely instructs women with short hair at their conversion (ladies of the night?) to let their hair grow out.

[24] Philipp Bachmann (*Der erste Brief des Paulus an die Korinther* [Kommentar zum Neuen Testament; Leipzig: A. Deichert (George Böhme), 1905] 356–59); Tischleder (*Wesen und Stellung*, 148–49), and James Moffatt (*The First Epistle of Paul to the Corinthians* [MNTC; New York and London: Harper, 1938] 152–53) argue that the man shames his head, Christ, by wearing a veil, inasmuch as he denies his participation in Christ's majesty. The woman shames her head, the man, by not wearing a veil, inasmuch as she denies her subordination to the "lordship" of the man. Similarly, see Jervell, *Imago Dei*, 304, and Bruce, *1 and 2 Corinthians*, 104. So too Héring: "The woman who presents herself bareheaded dishonors her husband, by wishing to be his equal. In some degree she is challenging his authority, by seeking to take a privilege reserved for him alone" (*First Epistle*, 105; see also p. 103). According to A. Feuillet ("L'homme 'gloire de Dieu' et la femme 'gloire de l'homme' [I Cor. XI. 7b]," *RB* 81 [1974] 174), she shames her husband merely by not conforming to expected social convention.

Gerhard Delling (*Paulus' Stellung*, 104) claims the head she shames is not her husband but her own head. Evans, (*Woman in the Bible*, 88–89) agrees. Weiss (*Der erste Korintherbrief*, 270–71) suggests vs 3 might be a gloss, and if so the references to "heads" in vss 4–6 could refer only to anatomical heads.

lowed by Greeks?[25] If not, is Paul here trying to impose a Jewish custom on Greeks,[26] a Greek custom on Jews,[27] or is he appealing to Greeks to conform to recognized conventions in their own society?[28]

> For a man ought not cover his head, inasmuch as he is the image and glory of God (εἰκὼν καὶ δόξα Θεοῦ ὑπάρχων), but the woman is the glory of a man (δόξα ἀνδρός ἐστιν). For man is not from woman, but woman from man, and man was not created for the sake of the woman, but woman for the sake of the man. (vss 7–9)

If, according to vs 3, the order of creation is God-Christ-man-woman, why does Paul here say the order is God-man-woman, thus omitting Christ? Why does a man's being "the image and glory of God" require him to uncover his head? Is it possible that Paul interpreted Genesis 1–3 as implying that only Adam, not Eve, was in the image of God?[29] Or does Paul indicate that the woman too is

---

[25] For discussions of Jewish and Greek uses of head coverings and hair styles see Str-B 3. 423–35; Delling, *Paulus' Stellung*, 96–109; Stefan Lösch, "Christliche Frauen in Corinth (1 Cor 11,2–16). Ein neuer Lösungsversuch," *ThQ* 127 (1947) 230–36; Hick, *Stellung des hl. Paulus*, 115–21; Héring, *First Epistle*, 109, n. 31; Annie Jaubert, "Le voile des femmes (1 Cor. XI. 2–16)," *NTS* 18 (1972) 424–27; Clark, *Man and Woman in Christ*, 168–69; Conzelmann, *1 Corinthians*, 184–86; esp. nn. 38–40 and 48; and Murphy-O'Connor, "Sex and Logic," 483–88.

[26] Leopold Zscharnack, *Der Dienst der Frau in den ersten Jahrhunderten der christlichen Kirche* (Göttingen: Vandenhoeck & Ruprecht, 1902) 67–68; D. Bornhäuser, "'Um der Engel willen' 1 Kor. 11,10," *NKZ* 41 (1930) 475–88; Delling, *Paulus' Stellung*, 96–98, 109; Werner George Kümmel in Hans Lietzmann, *An die Korinther I–II* (HNT 9; 4th ed.; Tübingen: Mohr-Siebeck, 1949) 183–84; Friedrich-Wilhelm Eltester, *Eikon im Neuen Testament* (BZNW 23; Berlin: Töpelmann, 1958) 153; André Rose, "L'épouse dans l'assemblée liturgique (I Cor. 11,2–16)," *BVC* 34 (1960) 15; Albrecht Oepke, "καλύπτω," *TDNT* 3 (1968) 561–63; Adinolfi, "Il velo della donna," 164 (so as not to offend Jews in the community); Klaus Thraede, "Ärger mit der Freiheit," 104–6; Thyen, "'... nicht mehr männlich und weiblich ...,'" 107–201; and Clark, *Man and Woman in Christ*, 169–70. Hick (*Stellung des hl. Paulus*, 115–21) claims the practice Paul desires conforms more to Jewish practice than Greek but not entirely to either.

[27] Padgett, "Paul on Women in the Church," 69–86.

[28] Most interpreters take this position. See, e.g., Conzelmann, *1 Corinthians*, 183–84. Isaksson (*Marriage and Ministry*, 166–85) argues that Paul is appealing neither to general Jewish nor to Greek conventions but to special rules for prophetesses.

[29] Zscharnack, *Der Dienst der Frau*, 4; Weiss, *Der erste Korintherbrief*, 272–73; Delling, *Paulus' Stellung*, 105–9; Leipoldt, *Die Frau*, 170–77; Jervell, *Imago Dei*, 296–301; Conzelmann, *1 Corinthians*, 182–88; Meier, "Veiling of Hermeneutics," 219; Thraede, "Ärger mit der Freiheit," 105; and Christoph Senft, *La première épître de saint-Paul aux Corinthiens* (CNT; 2d ser. 7; Neuchâtel: Delachaux & Niestlé, 1979) 142–43.

in God's image but is man's glory?[30] In what way is a woman "the glory of a man?"[31] Is this man her husband or men in general?[32]

For this reason the woman should have authority (ἐξουσία) [many MSS read: veil] on her head because of the angels. (vs 10)

What does "authority on her head" mean? Does it refer to the woman's own authority, to apotropaic magical power, or to the authority of the man over her?[33] Are these angels good or

---

[30] See Leenhardt, "La place de la femme," 17-20; Hick, *Stellung des hl. Paulus*, 124-29; Hooker, "Authority," 410-16; and Jaubert, "Le voile," 422-23; Feuillet, "'Gloire de Dieu,'" 175-77; Murphy-O'Connor, "Sex and Logic," 491-98; Thyen, "'... nicht mehr männlich und weiblich ...,'" 183-86; Clark, *Man and Woman in Christ*, 179; Bruce, *1 and 2 Corinthians*, 105; Hurley, *Man and Woman*, 171-74; Evans, *Woman in the Bible*, 86; and Schüssler Fiorenza, *In Memory of Her*, 229.

[31] Scholars generally understand "glory" to refer to a reflection or copy of the man's glory in the woman. However, Feuillet ("'Gloire de Dieu,'" 177-82) and others argue that the woman is man's glory not in the sense of derivative glory but in the positive sense of her being his honor, representing his dignity (see also her later article, "La dignité et le rôle de la femme d'après quelques textes pauliniens," *NTS* 21 [1975], esp. 159-62); Feuillet's discussion of the various meanings proposed for δόξα (glory) is helpful and thorough. See also Leenhardt, "La place de la femme," 17-20. Isaksson (*Marriage and Ministry*, 173-75) thinks "glory" here signifies the woman as the man's possession. M. Ginsburger ("La 'gloire' et l''autorité' de la femme dans I Cor. 11,1-10," *RHPhR* 12 [1932] 246-47) argues that Paul never intended to write "glory" (δόξα) but "resemblance" (δεῖγμα, or δόγμα), and was thinking in terms of a similar sounding Aramaic word (dyôqnāh). A Greek secretary, not familiar with this semitic meaning for δόγμα wrote δόξα.

[32] Most commentators understand the discussion to refer to men and women in general. Those who claim "man" refers to a woman's husband include Bachmann, *Der erste Brief*, 357; Isaksson, *Marriage and Ministry*, 174-75; Hurley, "Did Paul Require Veils?," 203; Rose, "L'épouse," 14; William F. Orr and James Arthur Walther, *I Corinthians* (AB 32; Garden City and New York: Doubleday, 1976) 264; and J. Duncan M. Derrett, "Religious Hair," in idem, *Studies in the New Testament* I: *Glimpses of the Legal and Social Presuppositions of the Authors* (Leiden: Brill, 1977) 172.

[33] Most commentators have thought the veil is a sign of her subordination to the man; see, e.g., Bachmann, *Der erste Brief*, 358, 361-63; Str-B 3. 435-36; Tischleder, *Wesen und Stellung*, 141-42; Delling, *Paulus' Stellung*, 101-3); Hick, *Stellung des hl. Paulus*, 131-34; C. Spicq, "Encore 'la puissance sur la tête,' (I Cor XI,10)," *RB* 48 (1939) 557-62; Werner Foerster, "ἔξεστιν," *TDNT* 2 (1964) 574; Clark, *Man and Woman in Christ*, 170-71; and Orr and Walther, *I Corinthians*, 263-64. Martin Dibelius (*Die Geisterwelt in Glauben des Paulus* [Göttingen: Vandenhoeck & Ruprecht, 1909] 16), however, argues it refers to a magical power given the woman and has nothing to do with her own authority or that of the man. He is followed by Weiss, *Der erste Korintherbrief*, 273-74; Weinel, *Paulus*, 202; Kümmel in Lietzmann, *An die*

malevolent?[34] What relationship does wearing a covering have to

Korinther, 184; Héring, First Epistle, 107–8; Schmithals, Gnosticism in Corinth, 242; Parvey, "Theology and Leadership," 126; and Conzelmann, 1 Corinthians, 188–90. According to Isaksson (Marriage and Ministry, 180–81), the authority is an emblem of some kind given the woman by her husband and the church allowing her to prophesy. Extrapolating from his extensive travels in Turkey, William Ramsay (The Cities of St. Paul: Their Influence on His Life and Thought [New York: A. C. Armstrong and Son; London: Hodder and Stoughton, 1907] 204) argued that the authority of the veil must be understood in light of the "Oriental" consideration of the veil as "the power and the honour and the dignity of the woman. With her veil on her head she can go anywhere in security and respect." So too Robertson and Plummer, First Epistle of St Paul to the Corinthians, 232–33; P. Rose "'Power on the Head,'" ExpTim 23 (1911/1912) 183–84; and Morris, First Epistle, 153–54.

For an excellent discussion of these positions see Joseph A. Fitzmyer, "A Feature of Qumrân Angelology and the Angels of 1 Cor 11:10," NTS 4 (1957) 50–53. Unfortunately, Fitzmyer ultimately sides with Gerhard Kittel's highly implausible suggestion that behind ἐξουσία (authority) is a word play on the Hebrew šilṭônayāh which can also mean "veil" (p. 53). As Fitzmyer himself recognized, this requires us to assume either that the Corinthians were Hebrew linguists as clever as Kittel or that Paul, for the sake of an esoteric pun, was willing to be misunderstood. Kittel's proposal appears in "Die 'Macht' auf dem Haupt (1 Cor XI.10),' Rabbinica (Religionsgeschichte des Urchristentums 1,3; Leipzig: Hinrichs, 1920) 17–31. See also J. Herklotz, "Zu 1 Kor. 11,10," BZ 10 (1912) 54; Ginsburger, "La 'gloire' et l'"autorité,'" 248; and Jervell, Imago Dei, 307–8. Vulnerable to the same objection are Günther Schwarz's proposal ("exousian echein epi tes kephales? [1 Korinther 11.10]," ZNW 70 [1979] 249) that ἐξουσία is a pun on the Aramaic ḥûmrā', and J. Duncan M. Derrett's ("Miscellanea: A Pauline Pun and Judas' Punishment," ZNW [1981] 131–33) that it puns on the Aramaic môrāh which can mean both "razor" and "authority."

According to Scroggs ("Paul and the Eschatological Woman," 301), "the head covering is what gives woman new freedom to be equal to man in the eschatological community." So too Hooker ("Authority," 414–16); Jaubert ("Le voile," 428–30); A. Feuillet, "Le signe de puissance sur la tête de la femme. 1 Co 11,10," NRTh 95 (1973) 945–54; and Jean Galot, Mission et ministère de la femme (Vie spirituelle et vie intérieure; Paris: Lethielleux, 1973) 123–25.

[34] The following view them as malevolent: Tert. De virginibus velandis 7; Weiss, Der erste Korintherbrief, 273–75; Lietzmann, An die Korinther, 54–55; Alfred Jeremias, "Der Schleier von Sumer bis Heute," Der alte Orient 31 (1931) 36; Ginsburger, "La 'gloire' et l'"autorité,'" 248; G. B. Caird, Principalities and Powers (Oxford: Oxford University Press, 1956) 17–20; Jervell, Imago Dei, 305–6; Schmithals, Gnosticism in Corinth, 242; Hurd, Origin of I Corinthians, 184, n. 4; and Parvey, "Theology and Leadership," 126.

The angels are viewed as good by the following: Bachmann, Der erste Brief, 363–66; Lyder Brun, "'Um der Engel willen' 1 Kor 11,10," ZNW 14 (1913) 303–8; Kittel, "Die 'Macht' auf dem Haupt," 26–30; Robertson and Plummer, First Epistle of St Paul to the Corinthians, 233; Spicq, "Encore 'la puissance,'" 562; E. B. Allo, Saint Paul: Première épître aux Corinthiens (2d ed.; Paris: Librairie Lecoffre, 1956) 261, 267; Hick, Stellung des hl. Paulus, 133–34; Tischleder, Wesen und Stellung, 158; Hooker, "Authority," 412–14; Isaksson, Marriage and Ministry, 177–78; Barrett, First

78   *Ritual, Sex, and Veils at Corinth*

angels? Does wearing it imitate the behavior of the worshipping angels of Isa 6:1–2?[35] Does it contain magical powers for warding off angelic attacks?[36] Does it hide or protect the woman from lecherous angels like the "Watchers" of Gen 6:1–4?[37] Does it symbolize a woman's subordination to her husband and thereby appease the angels responsible for maintaining the created order?[38] Does it symbolize the power that is hers through the protection of the angels who, present at creation, know she is the weaker gender?[39] Is it a token given her by her husband and the community acknowledging

Epistle, 253; Fitzmyer, "Qumrân Angelology," 55–58; Feuillet, "'Gloire de Dieu,'" 173–74; Adinolfi, "Il velo della donna," 172.

They are seen as potentially bad by: Dibelius, *Geisterwelt,* 17–22; Werner Foerster, "Zu I Cor 11.10," *ZNW* 30 (1931) 185–86; Kümmel, in Lietzmann, *An die Korinther,* 184; Leenhardt, "La place de la femme," 33, n. 16; Héring, *First Epistle,* 107–8; Conzelmann, *1 Corinthians,* 188–90.

Bornhäuser ("'Um der Engel willen,'" 478–84) denied the "angels" were supernatural; they were human "messengers" who would have been tempted by seeing women with heads uncovered. Similarly, see Padgett, "Paul on Women in the Church," 81–82.

[35] E.g., Konstantin Rösch, "'Um der Engel willen' (I Kor. XI,10)," *Theologie und Glaube* 24 (1932) 363–65; Ernest Evans, *The Epistles of the Apostle Paul to the Corinthians* (Clarendon Bible; Oxford: Oxford University Press, 1930) 116. This position is treated in Fitzmyer, "Qumrân Angelology," 53.

[36] Dibelius, *Geisterwelt,* 16; Kümmel, in Lietzmann, *An die Korinther,* 184; Leipoldt, *Die Frau,* 173; Schmithals, *Gnosticism in Corinth,* 242–43; Parvey, "Theology and Leadership," 126; Conzelmann, *1 Corinthians,* 188–90; and Senft, *La première épître,* 143–44.

[37] Leenhardt, "La place de la femme," 33, n. 16; Joseph Kürzinger, *Die Briefe des Apostels Paulus. Die Briefe an die Korinther und Galater* (Echter-Bible, Das neue Testament 6; Würzburg: Echter-Verlag, 1959) 28; Jervell, *Imago Dei,* 305–8; Thyen, "'... nicht mehr männlich und weiblich ...,'" 183. For a discussion of this position see Tischleder, *Wesen und Stellung,* 159–63. See *T. Reuben* 5:1–7; *Enoch* 6–7; 19:1; *Jub.* 4:22; 5:1–2; *2 Bar* 56:10–16; and Tob 6:14; 8:5.

[38] Bachmann, *Der erste Brief,* 363–66; Allo, *Saint Paul,* 266–67; Tischleder, *Wesen und Stellung,* 159; Str-B 3. 439; Joseph Sickenberger, *Die Briefe des heiligen Paulus an die Korinther und Römer* (Die heilige Schrift des Neuen Testaments 6; Bonn: Hanstein, 1932) 51; Spicq, "Encore 'la puissance,'" 562; Hick, *Stellung des hl. Paulus,* 131–34; Otto Kuss, *Die Briefe an die Römer, Korinther und Galater* (Das Neue Testament 6; Regensburg: Pustet, 1940) 164; Grosheide, *Commentary,* 257–58; Foerster, "ἔξεστιν," 574; Moffatt, *First Epistle,* 152–53; and Caird, *Principalities and Powers,* 18; Clark, *Man and Woman in Christ,* 170–71; Orr and Walther, *1 Corinthians,* 264; George W. Knight, *The New Testament Teaching on the Role Relationship of Men and Women* (Grand Rapids: Baker, 1977) 34; Peter Richardson, *Paul's Ethic of Freedom* (Philadelphia: Westminster, 1979) 65–66; and Derrett, "Religious Hair," 172.

[39] Brun, "'Um der Engel willen,'" 303–8; followed by R. St. John Parry, *The First Epistle of Paul the Apostle to the Corinthians* (Cambridge Greek New Testament; Cambridge: Cambridge University Press, 1916) 161.

that angels have spoken to her, which allows her to prophesy in public?[40] Does it compensate for some assumed bodily defect in the woman at which the angels present at worship might take offense?[41] Does it compensate for the woman's inferior status in creation and make her man's equal in worship with the angels?[42] Does it represent her intrinsic authority as a human over the spirit world?[43] Does it guarantee that she not offend angels at worship who "would be hostile to the radical distinction between the old and the eschatological orders" symbolized by removing the veil?[44] Does it educate the angels responsible for observing breaches in the Law that women now have authority to prophesy, an act forbidden in the order of creation?[45] Does it symbolize power granted her by the angels who mediate her prayers to God?[46] Does the elliptical brevity of this verse suggest it is a later interpolation and not from Paul's hand?[47]

Only in the Lord there is no woman without a man nor man without a woman.[48] For as the woman came from the man, so

---

[40] Isaksson, *Marriage and Ministry*, 180-81.

[41] Fitzmyer, "Qumrân Angelology," 55-58; and Henry J. Cadbury, "A Qumran Parallel to Paul," *HTR* 51 (1958) 1-2. For evidence of angels at worship see Ps 137 (138):1 (LXX); 1QSa 2:8-10; 1QSb; 4QMessa; 1QM 7:6; and Rev 8:3.

[42] Hooker, "Authority," 414-16; and Barrett, *First Epistle*, 253-55. Similarly, Jaubert, "Le voile," 430; Feuillet, "'Gloire de Dieu,'" 175-82; and idem, "Signe de puissance," 950-54; Rose, "L'épouse," 17; Bruce, *1 and 2 Corinthians*, 106; Galot, *Mission et ministère*, 123-26; and Grant R. Osborne, "Hermeneutics and Women in the Church," *JETS* 20 (1977) 342; and Longenecker, *New Testament Ethics for Today*, 81.

[43] Hurley, "Did Paul Require Veils?," 208-12; and idem, *Man and Woman*, 175-78.

[44] Scroggs, "Paul and the Eschatological Woman," 300, n. 46.

[45] Murphy-O'Connor, "Sex and Logic," 496-97.

[46] Schüssler Fiorenza, *In Memory of Her*, 228. Similarly, Adinolfi, "Il velo della donna," 172-73; and Howard Loewen, "The Pauline View of Women," *Direction* 6 (1977) 3-20.

[47] A. Jirku, "Die 'Macht' auf dem Haupt," *NKZ* 32 (1921) 711; and Clark, *Man and Woman in Christ*, 174. Other scholars have tried to explain διὰ τοὺς ἀγγέλους as a gloss or a corruption of something else. See, e.g., Richard Perdelwitz, "Die exousia auf dem Haupt der Frau," *Theologische Studien und Kritiken* 86 (1913) 611-13; and Feuillet, "Signe de puissance," 946.

[48] Josef Kürzinger ("Frau und Mann nach 1 Kor 11,11f," *BZ* 22 [1978] 270-75) argues that οὔτε . . . χωρίς, usually translated "there is no . . . without" or sometimes ". . . is nothing without" actually means "there is no distinction between. . . ." Although this meaning is possible, vs 12 suggests the issue is ontic interdependence not obliteration of distinctions.

also the man by means of a woman, and all things come from God. (vss 11-12)

What does Paul mean by "in the Lord?" Why would he try to prove that "in the Lord" men and women are equal by appealing to women's role in bearing male babies? Has Paul reversed his previous arguments here by claiming the order of creation and the order of childbearing somehow qualify each other?[49]

> Judge among yourselves: Is it fitting for a woman to pray to God uncovered? Does not nature herself teach us that if a man wears long hair it dishonors him, and if a woman wears long hair it is her glory? Long hair has been given to her for a garment (ἀντὶ περιβολαίου). (vss 13-15)

How does one best translate the phrase ἀντὶ περιβολαίου, rendered here "for a garment?" Inasmuch as it can also be translated "instead of a garment," does it suggest that the issue is hair styles, not head coverings? What is the force or cogency of Paul's argument from "nature"?

> And if someone seems to be quarrelsome . . . we have no such custom, nor do the churches of God. (vs 16)

Does this feeble appeal to conventions in other communities indicate that Paul sensed his other arguments lacked force?[50]

Several scholars have argued that the opaqueness, convolution, and apparent misogyny of 1 Cor 11:2-16 require one to attribute the passage to a later hand or hands; Paul himself, they argue, could not

[49] Kähler (*Frau*, 50-51) asserts that vss 3-10 are "corrected" here in vss 11-12. In the former, he argues from the order of creation; in the latter from "the order of redemption." See also Moffatt, *First Epistle*, 153; Scroggs, "Paul and the Eschatological Woman," 302; Schmithals, *Gnosticism in Corinth*, 240-43; and Conzelmann, *1 Corinthians*, 190. Feuillet ("'Gloire de Dieu,'" 175-82) thinks Paul has not reversed himself in vss 11-12 at all; rather, he has given the reader the proper context for understanding vss 3-10. So also Hick, *Stellung des hl. Paulus*, 126-29; and Evans, *Woman in the Bible*, 92. According to Isaksson (*Marriage and Ministry*, 182-83), Paul never had creation in mind at all. He simply meant that both men and women participate in procreation. Cf. *Gen. Rab.* 88.

[50] Weinel, *Paulus*, 202; J. C. B. Greig, "Women's Hats—1 Corinthians xi. 1-16," *ExpTim* 69 (1958) 156-57; Schmithals, *Gnosticism in Corinth*, 241; Conzelmann, *1 Corinthians*, 191; and Senft, *La première épître*, 145.

have written it. [51] Such attempts at literary surgery have met with little success and create as many problems as they solve. [52] In spite of its conundra and apparent inconsistencies with Paul's statements elsewhere, the passage is best considered integral to 1 Corinthians.

Perhaps the most fascinating but vexingly elusive question of all is "Why did Corinthian women uncover their heads in the first place?" Here the interpreter's imagination must take over; one must build a credible model for explaining this behavior using only the debris left us in Paul's demolition of it. If Paul's intentions are unclear, the Corinthians' are even more so. It therefore is not surprising that most commentators have skirted the issue, or have dismissed it with undefended conjectures. Were we to know the Corinthians' motivations, however, we could better unscramble Paul's messy denunciation. Jerome Murphy-O'Connor agrees:

> To a great extent the failure to perceive the force of Paul's logic has been due to a misunderstanding of the problem he was facing. If we can clarify this issue, it should be possible to see all the points he makes in their proper perspective. [53]

Even more important for our purposes, it should then be possible to see how the women's actions might relate to treading on "the garment of shame" and making "the male with the female neither male nor female."

Proposed Explanations
for Women's Altering Headcoverings

Scholars have proposed five explanations for the women's behavior. [54]

---

[51] William O. Walker, Jr., "1 Corinthians 11:2–16 and Paul's Views Regarding Women," *JBL* 94 (1975) 94–110; Lamar Cope, "1 Cor 11:2–16: One Step Further," *JBL* 97 (1978) 435 36; and G. W. Trompf, "On Attitudes Toward Women in Paul and Paulinist Literature: 1 Corinthians 11:3–16 and Its Context," *CBQ* 42 (1980) 196–215.

[52] See the criticisms of Walker by Murphy-O'Connor, "The Non-Pauline Character of 1 Corinthians 11:2–16?," *JBL* 95 (1976) 615–21.

[53] Murphy-O'Connor, "Sex and Logic," 483.

[54] Actually, there is also a sixth proposal, but one unworthy of scholarly attention. Alan Padgett claims the issue was hairstyles, not veils, and reconstructs affairs at Corinth like this:

> Paul, Priscilla, and possibly others with them during their stay in Corinth
> . . . do not wear their hair in the proper Greek manner. The Jews at the

1) According to the first, Corinthian women were simply resisting Paul's attempt to introduce Jewish fashions.[55] The artistic and literary evidence for Jewish and Greek head coverings is ambiguous; however, Greek practice clearly was more liberal. The veils of Greek women cascaded from the crown of the head over the hair, neck, and shoulders, but did not conceal the face. Unmarried women and maid servants were uncovered; married women in public customarily were covered, except in unusual situations.[56]

However, the veils of Jewish women—like those of near eastern women in general—often covered the face as well as the head, and were worn by married women whenever out-of-doors and sometimes even at home.[57] Even unmarried women usually wore them.[58] This stricter code among Jews implied that women unveiled were shameless and wanton.[59] A woman found in the street with unbound hair

---

Corinthian church, now thoroughly Hellenized, wear their hair in the Greek style in church, and the fact that Paul and his friends do not upsets them. ("Paul on Women in the Church," 77)

According to Padgett (ibid.), Paul repeats their arguments in 1 Cor 11:3–7b, namely that it is shameful for a woman not to have her hair piled up, and "corrects" them in 7c–16 by insisting that women have freedom (ἐξουσία) to wear their hair any way they wish—because of human messengers (διὰ τοὺς ἀγγέλους). But, what justification is there for identifying vss 3–7 as a quotation of the Corinthian position? Surely vs 3 indicates that vss 4–7 are Paul's own position: "But I want you to understand that. . . ." Padgett's interpretation is so forced, artificial, apologetic of Paul, and inattentive to basic exegetical matters that a careful reading of the text *eo ipso* is sufficient refutation.

[55] Evans, *The Epistles of the Apostle Paul to the Corinthians* (Clarendon Bible; Oxford: Oxford University Press, 1930) 115–16; A. Schlatter, *Die Korinthische Theologie* (BFCTh; Gütterloh: Bertelsmann, 1914) 23, and 54–55; Kümmel, in Lietzmann, *An die Korinther*, 183–84; Delling, *Paulus' Stellung*, 109; Thraede, "Ärger mit der Freiheit," 104–16; Thyen, "'. . . nicht mehr männliche und weiblich . . . ,'" 181–82.

[56] Plutarch *Questiones Romanae* 267a; and idem *Apophthegmata Laconia* 232c; Apuleius *The Golden Ass* 11.10; Vergil, *Aeneid* 7.524–25; Clem. Al. *Paid.* 3.11; *Martyrdom of Perpetua and Felicitas* 20. The first-century Roman historian Valerius Maximus (*Factorum ac dictorum memorabilium libri IX* 6.3.10) says that a certain "C. Sulpicius divorced his wife because he saw her going about in public with her head uncovered." See esp. R. and C. Kroeger, "Inquiry into Evidence of Maenadism."

[57] Philo *De spec. leg.* 3.56; and *Ketub.* 72a. See also *b. Yoma* 47a, where a woman brags that not even the beams of her home have seen her hair (Str-B 3. 430). Cf. *Sipre Num.* 5:18; *b. Ned.* 30b; *Giṭ.* 90a; *Num. Rab.* 9. On the other hand, the women depicted in the art of the Dura Europas synagogue, though veiled, have uncovered faces.

[58] *Exod. Rab.* 41:5.

[59] 3 Maccabees 4:6–10.

exposed could be summarily divorced.[60] According to Dio Chryso-stom, a younger contemporary of Paul, even the women in Tarsus, Paul's Hellenized home town, observed the eastern practice of cover-ing both head and face.[61]

To illustrate this hypothesis that the issue in Corinth was Greek resistance to Jewish custom, one could point to an analogous situa-tion in northern Africa at the end of the second century. Tertullian reveals that pagan married women in north Africa veiled themselves in public but virgins went about unveiled.[62] Some Christian virgins also were unveiled, while others, in the interests of modesty, volun-tarily chose to veil themselves.[63] This freedom of virigins to accept or reject the veil caused resentment among some married women who likewise wanted the freedom to be unveiled in church.[64] Tertullian's response to this pastoral problem was to insist that all women after puberty, virgins and matrons, always be veiled in public in accord with Jewish practice. This, he argues, was also the practice of churches in Greece, Asia Minor, and in some areas of Africa.[65]

Clement of Alexandria also expected women to veil their heads and faces whenever in public.

> Let her be entirely covered unless at home. For that style of dress is grave, and protects from being gazed at. And she will never fall, who puts before her eyes modesty, and her shawl; nor will she invite another to fall into sin by covering her face.[66]

From the perspective of these parallels it might indeed appear that Corinthian women resented the imposition of Jewish fashions. Paul, on the other hand, as a Jew and a Tarsian, would have expected all holy women to veil themselves. However, this hypothesis fails to explain the situation fully.

Surely some of the Corinthians were themselves Jewish; if so, Paul would be siding with Jewish women against Greeks. There is no evidence of this schism in the text or anywhere else in 1 Corinthians. In fact, Paul repeatedly appeals to universal—not dis-tinctively Jewish—attitudes toward "shameful" fashions (vss 4–6

---

[60] *m. Ketub.* 7:6; cf. 5:8 and *t. Soṭa* 5:9.
[61] *Discourse* 33, 48.
[62] *De virginibus velandis,* 2–13.
[63] Ibid., 3.
[64] Ibid.
[65] Ibid., 2.
[66] *Paid.* 3.11.

and 14–15) and appropriate dress (vs 13: "Judge among yourselves; is it fitting . . .?"). Furthermore, vs 16 makes clear that the
practice he wants the Corinthians to observe obtains in all other
Greek churches; why only in Corinth did this practice meet resistance?
There is, however, an even more telling objection to this
hypothesis. The women seem to have deviated from general practice
only when praying and prophesying. If we take Paul's language
strictly, they came to the public meeting covered, remained covered
except when actively participating, and presumably went home
covered. Paul's primary complaint with their worship is that at these
particular moments the women have blurred the "natural" distinctions between their appearances and the men's. Surely it is unlikely
that these women objected to the imposition of Jewish customs only
when praying and prophesying.
One aspect of this interpretation, however, merits praise. It
rightly recognizes that the issue Paul addresses pertains primarily to
women: Paul mentions men's short hair and uncovered heads only
for purposes of distinguishing their appearance from women's long
hair and headcoverings. There is no good reason to think that men
did in fact cover their heads.

2) According to Heinrich Weinel, Corinthian women had adopted
without complaint Jewish veils that covered not only the head but
the nose and mouth as well, thus hampering speech. The women
removed them not out of protest but merely to be more articulate
when praying and prophesying.[67]
This explanation too is implausible. Surely the women need not
have removed their veils completely in order to uncover their
mouths. Paul does not demand a covering on the face (πρόσωπον)
or mouth (στόμα) but on the head (κεφαλή).

3) Stefan Lösch cited two Peleponnesian inscriptions as evidence that
certain Greek cults prohibited women from participating in proces-
sions or entering the temple with braided hair or veiled heads,
inasmuch as braids and veils were considered pretentious and
irreverent.[68] Lösch further suggested that some of the Corinthian
women, once priestesses in just such cults, unveiled their heads in

---

[67] Weinel, *Paulus*, 202. For a refutation of this position see Leipoldt, *Die Frau*, 264,
n. 10.
[68] Stefan Lösch, "Christliche Frauen in Corinth (1 Cor 11,2–16). Ein neuer
Lösungsversuch," *ThQ* 127 (1947) 216–61.

worship as a natural continuation of former pious practice. Paul's adamancy that women observe Jewish veiling customs in worship issued from his fear that they might lapse into paganism. Lösch also claimed that the "authority on her head" in 1 Cor 11:10 refers to a σπλεγγίς, also mentioned in one of the inscriptions, which apparently was a hair ornament worn only when hair was braided or knotted and symbolized a woman's subjection to her husband. Though ingenious and in many respects attractive, this hypothesis too fails. The inscriptions forbid only braided hair, not veils, unless one agrees with Lösch's unnecessary emendation of the Arcadian inscription. Unemended, it prohibits a *man* from entering the temple "covered." Furthermore, if one were to press for consistency between the behavior depicted in the inscriptions and the behavior of women at Corinth, we would expect the women not to have unbraided their hair only when praying or prophesying but to have come to the gathering with hair unbraided already. More objectionable is Lösch's failure to make Paul's theological argumentation directly germane to the women's motivations for removing their veils or to explain why Paul would have mentioned "the angels" in connection with a woman wearing a σπλεγγίς/ἐξουσία.

4) Elisabeth Schüssler Fiorenza too proposes that Greco-Roman religious convention influenced Corinthian women, but in her proposal—developing an earlier suggestion by R. and C. Kroeger—the issue was not veils but hairstyles, and the motivation not sartorial simplicity but corybantic ecstacy:

> During their ecstatic-pneumatic worship celebrations some of the Corinthian women prophets and liturgists unbound their hair, letting it flow freely rather than keeping it in fashionable coiffure. . . . Such ecstatic frenzy in oriental cults was a highly desirable spiritual phenomenon and a mark of true prophecy. Disheveled hair and head thrown back were typical for the maenads in the cult of Dionysos, in that of Cybele, the Pythia at Delphi, the Sibyl, and unbound hair was necessary for a woman to produce an effective magical incantation.
>
> Flowing and unbound hair was also found in the Isis cult, which had a major center in Corinth. For instance, a woman friend of the poet Tibullus is said to have had to let her hair down twice daily in the worship of Isis to "say lauds."
>
> The Corinthian pneumatics presumably took over such a fashion because they understood their equality in community and their devotion to Sophia-Spirit by analogy to the worship of Isis, since

Isis was also said to have made the power of women equal to men. . . . Paul, on the other hand, is bent on curbing the pneumatic frenzy of the Corinthians' worship. For Paul, building up of the community and intelligible missionary proclamation, not orgiastic behavior, are the true signs of the spirit. In this context it is understandable why Paul insists that women should keep their hair bound up.[69]

Schüssler Fiorenza rightly relates the practice to Corinthian enthusiastic worship. In the chapters immediately following, Paul addresses the Corinthians' public rituals and by so doing reveals how prayer and prophecy were conducted there. Prayer at Corinth seems virtually synonymous with glossalalia. This manifestation of "tongues of angels" (13:1) included praying "in the spirit," singing "in the spirit," and blessing "in the spirit" (14:15–16), which Paul contrasts with praying, singing, and giving thanks "in the mind," that is, in articulate and intelligible discourse (14:14–16). These ecstatic utterances of "mysteries in the spirit" (14:2) were so wild that Paul feared outsiders would think them mad (14:23).

Paul distinguishes prophecy from glossalalia, claiming that whereas tongues is speaking to God and self-edifying (14:2, 4), prophecy is speaking to other humans and edifying to them (14:3–4). He implies that prophecy was not so enthusiastic as prayer, but a closer reading shows that prophecy too was unruly. Several prophets spoke in the assembly simultaneously, causing confusion (14:29–33). Paul's insistence that "the spirits of prophets are subject to prophets" surely is directed against those who claimed to have been moved solely by the divine spirit (14:32). The Corinthians indeed were "eager for manifestations of the spirit" (14:12). Therefore, when Paul speaks in 1 Corinthians 11 of women praying and prophesying, he probably had in mind precisely such frenzied activity.[70]

However, Schüssler Fiorenza errs in supposing that in such worship women let down their hair. The most natural reading of the text suggests they removed veils, and this is how most ancient interpreters understood it. Many early manuscripts in fact read "veil"

---

[69] Schüssler Fiorenza, *In Memory of Her*, 227–28; R. and C. Kroeger, "Inquiry into Evidence of Maenadism," 331–38. Similarly, see Isaksson (*Marriage and Ministry*, 169), though he also claims the women let down their hair to symbolize their presenting themselves to God as brides.

[70] I consider unworthy of comment Noel Weeks' proposal that the women in Corinth were praying by means of being uncovered ("On Silence and Head Covering," *WTJ* 35 [1972] 25–27).

(κάλυμμα, or in Latin *velamen*) in place of "authority" (ἐξουσία, vs 10). The clever lexical arguments used for claiming the issue is hairstyles fail to accomplish that which their champions want. Even if one granted—and I do not—that the phrase "having something on his head" (κατὰ κεφαλῆς ἔχων, vs 4) is best rendered "having something descending from his head," it surely could apply to veils which also descended from one's pate.[71] The argument that the phrase "for a garment" (ἀντὶ περιβολαίου, vs 15) must be translated "instead of a garment" surrenders before an army of uses in which ἀντί best means "for," "as," or "equivalent to."[72] Hair is "like a garment," not "in place of a garment." When Paul refers to hair lengths in vss 14–15 he does so not because hair itself was at issue but in order to argue by analogy. Nature has supplied woman with a natural "garment," her long hair. What nature began let women complete by retaining fabric garments on their heads.[73] Even if "covering" could refer to hair piled up in a bun, it is more natural to make it refer to veils which cover the head more completely. Paul compares a woman "uncovered" to one shorn (vss 5–6) and to the appearance of a man (14–15). Surely women with hair tightly arranged—as was the rule[74]—but unveiled look balder and more like men than those with hair unfurled and aswirl in corybantic frenzy. When pressed for consistency, this proposal becomes absurd: vs 7 would then read "for a man ought not have his hair piled up in a bun."

5) The fifth hypothesis advanced for explaining the behavior of Corinthian women is by far the most common, and it almost invariably involves Gal 3:28. For example, Archibald Robertson and Alfred Plummer suggest the women "argued that distinctions of sexes were done away in Christ (Gal iii, 28), and that it was not seemly that a mark of servitude should be worn in Christian worship."[75] According to P. Tischleder, the Corinthian women had an

---

[71] The same phrase appears in Plutarch (*Regum et imperatorum apophthegmata*, 13) and clearly refers to a garment (κατὰ τῆς κεφαλῆς ἔχων τὸ ἱμάτιον).

[72] See LSJ, 153; and BAG, 73.

[73] See Meier, "Veiling of Hermeneutics," 222–23.

[74] See W. C. Van Unnik, "Les chevaux défaits des femmes baptisées. Un rite de baptême dans l'ordre ecclésiastique d'Hippolyte," *VC* 1 (1947) 87–88. Cf. Clem. Al. *Paid.* 3.11.

[75] Robertson and Plummer, *First Epistle of St Paul to the Corinthians*, 230. See also Zscharnack, *Der Dienst der Frau*, 67; Bachmann, *Der erste Brief*, 355–57, 366; Bornhäuser, "'Um der Engel willen,'" 482–83; Weiss, *Der erste Korintherbrief*, 268–69; Brun, "'Um der Engel willen,'" 302–3; Leenhardt, "La place de la

"ill-timed and dangerous lust for emancipation."[76] Jean Héring too attributes the practice to "feminist tendencies."[77] Scholars who hold this position, however, disagree concerning the source of this feminism. According to John P. Meier, "the ultimate cause of the revolt" was Paul himself:

> If Paul had told the Christians at Corinth, as he told the Christians in Galatia, that in Christ "there is neither male nor female" . . . then the unveiled women . . . might feel they were simply taking Paul at his word and putting the Christian gospel of freedom into practice.[78]

According to Franz Leenhardt, Paul was only indirectly responsible. Corinthian women took over the "slogan" Galatian women used to express their new freedom in Christ and extended its relevance to decry the wearing of veils in worship.[79]

Wayne Meeks and Jerome Murphy-O'Connor suggest that Paul cannot be blamed inasmuch as the Corinthians filtered Gal 3:28 through their un-Pauline "realized eschatology" which for them

---

femme," 22–23, 31; Spicq, "Encore 'la puissance,'" 557, 560; T. C. Craig, "The First Epistle to the Corinthians," *IB* 10. 125; Leipoldt, *Die Frau*, 171–72 (who likens the removal of veils to German women taking up smoking in the 1920's); Jervell, *Imago Dei*, 294–95; Joseph Kürzinger, *Die Briefe des Apostels Paulus. Die Briefe an die Korinther und Galater* (Echter-Bible, Das neue Testament 6; Würzburg: Echter-Verlag, 1959) 28; Grosheide, *Commentary*, 250, 258; Morris, *First Epistle*, 151; Philippe-H. Menoud, "Saint Paul et la femme," *RThPh* 19 (1969) 323–24; J. Ruef, *Paul's First Letter to Corinth* (Westminster Pelican Commentaries; Philadelphia: Westminster; London: SCM, 1977) 109; Hurley, "Did Paul Require Veils?," 200–201; and idem, *Man and Woman*, 171, 177; Russell P. Spittler, *The Corinthian Correspondence* (Springfield, Missouri: Gospel Publishing House, 1976) 52–58; George W. Knight, *The New Testament Teaching on the Role Relationship of Men and Women* (Grand Rapids: Baker, 1977) 32; Derrett, "Religious Hair," 171; Bruce K. Waltke, "1 Corinthians 11,2–16: An Interpretation," *BSac* 135 (1978) 46; Robert Jewett, "Sexual Liberation of the Apostle Paul," 67; Evans, *Woman in the Bible*, 94; and Longenecker, *New Testament Ethics for Today*, 79–80. Hick (*Stellung des hl. Paulus*, 118–21) combines this explanation with the first—i.e., Greek resistance to Jewish custom—claiming that some women were feminists, some Greek conservatives.

[76] Tischleder, *Wesen und Stellung*, 156; similarly, Richard Perdelwitz, "Die exousia auf dem Haupt der Frau," *Theologische Studien und Kritiken* 86 (1913) 612; and Allo, *Saint Paul*, 254, 258.

[77] Héring, *First Epistle*, 102. See also Barrett, *First Epistle*, 247.

[78] Meier, "Veiling of Hermeneutics," 217.

[79] Leenhardt, "La place de la femme," 31.

included the unity of the sexes.[80] "If there was no longer any male or female, the Corinthians felt free to blur the distinctions between the sexes."[81]

Else Kähler, Walther Schmithals, Otto Bangerter, and Constance Parvey think that the removal of veils characterized a Gnostic circle at Corinth demanding women's liberation.[82] As Schmithals expresses it, the liberation of women was a necessary consequence of their freedom from "the sphere of the *sarx*" which had been divided into sexes. "If the Pneuma is the real self ... then the person ... is neither male nor female."[83]

There can be little doubt that women could have interpreted the removal of veils as an act of sexual liberation. Like most cultural symbols, the veil is a complex of meanings and associations and veiling practices varied dramatically from culture to culture, from region to region, from class to class, and from time to time. Consequently, it is difficult to know precisely what practice characterized first-century Corinth, not to mention a sect influenced by foreign, that is, Jewish customs. This imprecision together with the internal confusion of 1 Cor 11:2–16 has made it an exegetical Rorschach test. Often the responses to Paul's ink blots have revealed little more than the imaginative powers and penchants of the interpreter.

But in spite of the wide diversity of actual veiling practices, the veil consistently represented a woman's inferiority and subordination and was used by Jews, Greeks, Romans, and Christians as an effective form of social control. According to Roland De Vaux, the veil in the ancient near east, including ancient Israel, made clear to others that a woman was the property of her father or husband, thus protecting male rights.[84]

In hellenized Judaism too women were considered under the authority of their husbands:

[80] Meeks, "Image of the Androgyne," 202; and Murphy-O'Connor, "Sex and Logic," 490. See also Derwood C. Smith, "Paul and the Non-Eschatological Woman," *Ohio Journal of Religious Studies* 4 (1976) 17.

[81] Murphy-O'Connor, "Sex and Logic," 490.

[82] Kähler, *Frau*, 50; Schmithals, *Gnosticism in Corinth*, 239; Bangerter, *Frauen im Aufbruch. Die Geschichte einer Frauenbewegung in der Alten Kirche. Ein Beitrag zur Frauenfrage* (Neukirchen-Vluyn: Neukirchener Verlag, 1971) 33–35; and Parvey, "Theology and Leadership," 124–25.

[83] Schmithals, *Gnosticism in Corinth*, 239; similarly, Senft, *La première épître*, 141.

[84] De Vaux, "Sur le voile des femmes dans l'Orient ancien," *RB* 44 (1936) 411–12.

The woman, says the Law, is in all things inferior to the man. Let her accordingly be submissive, not that she be sexually violated by the man, but that she be ruled; for God gave the power to her husband. [85]

Veils were considered evidence that women were under a man's authority [86] and emblems of modesty shielding women from men's gazes. [87] Consequently, women without veils were considered shameless. [88] So too in rabbinic Judaism:

Why does a man go about bareheaded while a woman goes out with her head covered? She is like one who has done wrong and is ashamed of people: therefore she goes out with her head covered. [89]

Conversely, a man's uncovered head symbolized his freedom. [90]

Even though veiling practices were more liberal among non-Jews, here too a woman's assumed inferiority to a man rendered the veil an emblem of shame. [91] According to Tertullian a veil was a token of modesty when worn by virgins, [92] and a token of the loss of virginity when worn by matrons. [93] In either case, it symbolized a woman's inferiority.

I pray you, be you mother, or sister, or virgin-daughter . . . veil your head: if a mother, for your sons' sakes; if a sister, for your brethren's sakes; if a daughter for your fathers' sakes. All ages are periled in your person. Put on the panoply of modesty; surround yourself with the stockade of bashfulness; rear a rampart for your sex, which must neither allow your own eyes egress nor ingress to other people's. Wear the full garb of matron, to preserve the standing of virgin. . . . For wedded you are to Christ: to Him you have surrendered your flesh; to Him you have espoused your maturity. Walk in accordance with the will

---

[85] Josephus *Contra Apionem* 2.200–201.

[86] See Str-B 3. 435–39.

[87] Philo *De spec. leg.* 3.56. Cf. Gen 24:65.

[88] 3 Maccabees 4:6–10.

[89] *Ber. Rab.* 17:8, as quoted in Parvey, "Theology and Leadership," 125–26.

[90] Jaubert, "Le voile," 421–23. See *Exod. Rab.* 18:10; *Tg. Onq.* on Exod 14:8, and on Judg 5:9.

[91] Aristophanes *Lysistrata* 326–33.

[92] *De virginibus velandis* 8–17. See also *Didascalia Apostolorum* 3; and Jerome, *Letter 22, To Eustochium* 25.

[93] *De virginibus velandis* 3, 11.

of your Espoused. Christ is He who bids the espoused and wives of others veil themselves; (and) of course, much more His own.[94]

Tertullian's misogyny, though more articulate than that of most early Christian authors, is not unique. In the *Acts of Thomas* women who go about in the world bareheaded are shameless and will suffer in hell by being hung by the hair.[95] The *Shepherd of Hermas* depicts demonic women with heads unveiled and hair unfastened.[96]

It would appear then that among Jews, pagans, and Christians the veil was distinctive female attire, and symbolized modesty, loss of virginity (veiling of married women was more rigid), and subordination to a father or husband. In the androcentric cultures of antiquity, this complex of associations presupposed and reinforced woman's inferiority. The veil was hardly a woman's glory, as Paul would have us think.

Conversely, an unveiled head was identified with male attire. In the case of younger women it usually represented virginity, but the unveiling of older women implied immodest independence or even wantonness. Whatever else might be said concerning veils in antiquity, their removal could symbolize a revolutionary change in a woman's sexual and social status.

However, the hypothesis that Corinthian women removed their veils out of "a lust for emancipation," like the other hypotheses, fails fully to account for the activity opposed in 1 Corinthians 11. Why would women have removed their veils only when actively speaking in worship? They seem to have had no objection to wearing veils, their cultural symbols of submission, at other times. If they were such adamant feminists one might suppose they would have remained uncovered forever. Surely it is more likely that they considered ecstatic worship a suspension of one's normal condition, as a momentary denial of mortal contingencies, as a liminal event in which one achieved a more perfect ontology.[97] If so, it would be helpful to know more precisely what they might have understood this ritually achieved ontology to be.

[94] Ibid., 16.
[95] *Acts Thom.* 56.
[96] *Herm. Sim.* 9.9, 15.
[97] So also Senft, *La première épître*, 141.

The Cultic Return to the
Divine Image at Corinth

Without question the most obstreperous verse in 1 Cor 11:2–16 is vs 10: "For this reason a woman should have an authority on her head because of the angels." The problem is that there is no parallel in Greek for ἐξουσία (authority) representing a veil, and there is no clear indication why angels should figure into the discussion here. On the other hand, this verse is the most crucial inasmuch as it caps off Paul's argument. The presence of διὰ τοῦτο (for this reason) shows that it continues the argument from creation in vss 3–9, while vs 11 abruptly begins a new idea. Why is Paul so obscure at the apex of his discussion?

I suggest that the Corinthians would not have thought Paul obscure at all. The women had removed their veils in worship for the very purpose of dramatizing their authority over the angels, and they did so because of their reading of Genesis 1–3.

It is clear that Genesis 1–2 is at the heart of Paul's argument. At the beginning, he gives his own understanding of the order of creation (vs 3), in the middle of the argument he discusses Gen 1:26–27 and Gen 2:18–24 (vss 7–9), and returns to creation in vs 11. According to Jervell, the fact that Paul's discussion of the divine image in this passage is entirely foreign to his usual understanding of Genesis 1–3 suggests that it was framed as a specific response to a rival interpretation of primeval history.[98]

The Corinthians did indeed have a rival interpretation of primeval history. As we have seen, they, like Philo, divided the creation accounts into a sequential two-staged creation of the human. We know this from 1 Cor 15:45–49 where Paul awkwardly debates it. The first human was "spiritual" (πνευματικός), "from heaven" (ἐξ οὐρανοῦ), and therefore "heavenly" (ἐπουράνιος). The second human was "psychic" (ψυχικός), "from the clay of earth" (ἐκ γῆς χοϊκός), and therefore "clayish" (χοϊκός). Although Paul does not say so explicitly, the parallels in Philo and elsewhere suggest that the Corinthians also may have assumed that the heavenly human was sexually unified; the earthly human sexually divided. Apparently they called the natural human state "wearing the image of the man of clay" and their own transcendent condition "wearing the image of the man of heaven."

---

[98] Jervell, *Imago Dei*, 295.

These "spirituals" thought they had special authority as the result of having attained the image of the first human. In all of Paul's writings the word ἐξουσία (authority) appears seventeen times, twelve of these in his letters to Corinth; of these twelve ten appear in 1 Corinthians. The cognate verb ἔξεστι (it is permitted) occurs five times in Paul, all in letters to Corinth, all but one in 1 Corinthians. The verb ἐξουσιάζω (I bring under authority) occurs three times, all in 1 Corinthians. The Corinthians in fact had a slogan that Paul quotes four times: "all things are permissible to me," or "I have authority to do anything" (1 Cor 6:12; 10:23—cited twice in each). There can be little doubt that freedom and its limits were central to the conflict between Paul and these pneumatics. Therefore it is significant that when Paul tells women to cover their heads he refers to the covering using their own catchword: "authority" (ἐξουσία).

Furthermore, the Corinthians apparently claimed their exalted status resulted in invulnerability with respect to the spirit world. In 15:22–28, once again referring to Adam, Paul insists that it is only in the eschaton that believers can claim victory over the spirit world:

> Then comes the end, when he delivers the kingdom to God the Father after destroying every rule and every authority and power. For he must reign until he has put all his enemies under his feet. The last enemy to be destroyed is death. "For God has put all things in subjection under his feet." (vss 24–27)

Paul may be ridiculing the Corinthians' claim to have achieved authority over the angels when he says "Already you rule!" (4:8). Paul's own status, however, is "last of all . . . a spectacle . . . to angels" (4:9).

In order better to understand the relationship of authority over angels to the divine image we must examine in more detail contemporary interpretations of Genesis. According to Gen 1:26–28, God's image granted Adam "dominion over the fish of the sea and over the birds of the air, and over the cattle, and over all the earth, and over every creeping thing that creeps upon the earth" (vs 26).[99]

---

[99] The LXX uses the words ἄρχω and κατακυριεύω to express this power over creation. Cf. Ps 8:4–9 (LXX) where the human is placed just under the angels in authority. Sir 17:1–6 in the Greek version says God gave the human in his image ἐξουσία, ἰσχύς, and φόβος over all creation in order to "dominate beasts and flying things." See also Wis 9:1–3; 1QS 3.17–18; 2 Enoch 30:10–12; 31:2–4; 58:3; 4 Ezra 6:54; Jub. 2:14; 2 Bar. 14:18; Gen. Rab. 23:6 (= 24:6); The Letter to Diognetus 10:2; and esp.

Rabbinic interpreters supposed that this authority of the image extended to domination over angels as well, who, it was claimed, were created on day one, or two, or as late as day five, along with the "swarms of living creatures," "birds," and "great sea monsters." [100] Traces of this connection between the image of God and authority over the angels appear already in Hellenistic Judaism. [101] According to *The Life of Adam and Eve*, Satan and the demons lost their angelic glory because they refused to worship the image of God, that is, Adam. After all, they had been created before Adam (12-15; cf. 37-39). Likewise, in *The Apocalypse of Moses* Eve rebukes the serpent for having bitten Seth: "Thou wicked beast, fearest thou not to fight with the image of God? . . . How didst thou not call to mind thy subjection? For long ago was thou made subject to the image of God?" (10:3).

Strictly speaking, in these two documents only the men, Adam and Seth, are said to be in God's image and worthy of the angels' veneration (cf. Gen 5:1-2). Some rabbis claimed that male vulnerability to angels began with Enoch. [102] However, Philo would have argued that this vulnerability began already when God created the "man of clay" (Gen 2:7), who was not created in God's image and who was not given authority to rule the world.

Eve's situation, however, was otherwise. She was vulnerable to the spirit world from the beginning; were this not the case, she would not have been beguiled by the serpent. Her vulnerability was due to her not being fully participant in God's image. Whatever freedom she did once enjoy she lost at her fall. According to Philo, she thereby lost her freedom (ἐλευθερία) and came under the domination (δεσποτεία) of her husband. [103]

Among the curses on Eve, the rabbis included the wearing of a veil. For example, in *Pirqe R. El.* 14 and ʾ*Abot R. Nat.* B 9:25

Deut. Rab. 4:4. *Ep. Barn.* 6:8-19 speaks of Adam's ἐξουσία over all things. Philo (*De Mos.*, 2.65) states that God's image is related to "hegemony" and "power" over everything related to the earth. The Gnostic treatise *On the Origin of the World* relates Adam's glory to his potential for ruling even God and the angels who had created him ([NHC 2, 5] 120.128-121.14). See also Jervell, *Imago Dei*, 37-41, 88-90.

[100] See Louis Ginzberg, *Legends of the Jews*, 5. 20-25.

[101] For evidence that Adam was created to be like angels see *1 Enoch* 69:11; *2 Enoch* 30:10-12; and *Mek. Beshalla* 7:73-80. According to Sir 25:24 (LXX) all women should be denied ἐξουσία because of Eve's sin.

[102] *Gen. Rab.* 23:6 (= 24:6).

[103] *De op. mun.* 167.

and 42:117 women are required to wear a veil as a sign of mourning
for Eve's sin.

> Why does Woman cover her head and man not cover his head?
> A parable. To what may this be compared? To a woman who
> disgraced herself and because she disgraced herself, she is
> ashamed in the presence of people. In the same way Eve dis-
> graced herself and caused her daughters to cover their heads.
> (9:25)

Also in *b.* ʿ*Erubin* 100b Eve's curse resulted in women's being
"wrapped up like a mourner, banished from the company of all
men."[104]

The veil as a sign of mourning for Eve's sin was current also
among early Christians. Tertullian tells women to be attired

> as Eve mourning and repentant, in order that by every garb of
> penitence she might the more fully expiate that which she
> derives from Eve,—the ignominy, I mean, of the first sin, and
> the odium (attaching to her as the cause) of human perdition.
> ... And do you not know that you are (each) an Eve? The
> sentence of God on this sex of yours lives in the age: the guilt
> must of necessity live too. You are the devil's gateway: you are
> the unsealer of that (forbidden) tree: you are the first deserter
> of the divine law: you are she who persuaded him whom the
> devil was not valiant enough to attack. You destroyed so easily
> God's image, man. On account of your desert—that is, death—
> even the Son of God had to die.[105]

It would therefore appear that the Corinthian order of creation
was: (1) God; (2) the pneumatic, sexually unified *Urmensch*, who, by
dint of the image of God, enjoyed hegemony over the spirit world;
(3) the psychic, sexually divided human made out of clay according
to Gen 2:7, no longer in God's image and therefore not sovereign
over angels; and (4) Eve, whose fall women mourn by wearing veils.
If this is more or less their interpretation of Genesis 1–3, their
return to the divine image might well have been symbolized by
women's removing their veils. They compensated for Eve's sin by
climbing a rung on the ladder of being, by reuniting the primordial
androgyne, and thereby enjoying "authority because of the angels."

[104] See also ʾ*Abot R. Nat.* A 1. For veils used in mourning see Str-B 3. 430. See
also *b. Moʿed Qaṭ.* 15, 24; and *Pirqe R. El.* 17.
[105] *De cultus feminarum* 1:1. Cf. *Adv. Marc.* 5:8, and *De oratione* 22.

But why did they symbolize this in acts of ecstatic worship? Hermann Baumann, an ethnological expert in ritual transvestism, argues that because garments are extensions of one's personality and ontology, changes in garments are common in religious rites associated with ontic changes.[106] The exchange of garments in early Christian baptisms is a good example. Baumann also claims that in cultures understanding the human essence—say, soul or spirit—to be sexually unified, or the deity to be asexual or bisexual, the cultic participant sometimes dons attire of the opposite sex in order to symbolize attainment of the power of the soul or the deity, a power often including protection from the spirit world.[107] This, I suggest, is precisely what happened at Corinth.

One story from antiquity graphically illustrates the cultic implications of women becoming male and removing their veils of shame. *Joseph and Asenath,* a Jewish romance, probably Alexandrian,[108] and written sometime between the translation of the Greek Old Testament and Hadrian's edict against Jewish proselytizing,[109] in other words, from two centuries before to less than a century after Paul.

The story—elements of which are unquestionably traditional—explains how it was that the patriarch Joseph married a non-Jew, the daughter of a pagan priest![110] Presumably, Asenath served as the paradigmatic convert, a model of how gentiles, especially gentile women, should become Jews.

When Asenath first meets Joseph she wears an expensive robe, jewelry engraved with the names of Egyptian deities, and several layers of head coverings: a tiara, a diadem, and a veil (3:10–11). Later, she abandons her gods, takes off her robe and head coverings, puts on sackcloth and ashes, fasts for seven days, and prays that God

---

[106] Baumann, *Das doppelte Geschlecht,* 46. Ernest Crawley also discusses ritual transvestism in *Dress, Drinks, and Drums.* See also Eliade, *Mephistopheles and the Androgyne: Studies in Religious Myth and Symbol* (New York: Sheed and Ward, 1965) 78–124. W. C. Van Unnik has collected evidence from ancient sources in which women ritually let down their hair and removed jewelry. His explanation ("Les cheveux défaits," 77–100) that Christian women did so in baptism to symbolize repentance and to allow water to penetrate their hairdos probably is too rationalistic.

[107] Baumann, *Das doppelte Geschlecht,* 45–57.

[108] Christoph Burchard, *Untersuchungen zu Joseph und Asenath: Überlieferung, Ortsbestimmung* (WUNT 8; Tübingen: Mohr-Siebeck, 1965) 142–43.

[109] Burchard (*Untersuchungen,* 143–48) dates it to the first century BCE. See also Howard Clark Kee, "The Socio-Religious Setting and Aims of 'Joseph and Asenath,'" in George W. MacRae, ed., *Society of Biblical Literature 1976 Seminar Papers* (Missoula: Scholars Press, 1976) 190.

[110] Gen 41:45.

may protect her from the devil and his servants, the Egyptian gods (12:9–10). At dawn on the eighth day Michael appears and tells her to put off her black garment, shake the ashes from her head, wash her face in living water, put on a new untouched robe, and gird her loins with a double girdle of virginity (14:13). All this she does, but in addition she covers her head with a veil (14:17). Michael immediately commands her to remove the veil, "because today you are a pure virgin and your head is like that of a young man" (15:1). After she removes it, he tells her: "From today you will be renewed, remolded and made alive once more, and you will eat the bread of life and drink the cup of immortality and be anointed with the chrism of incorruption" (15:4). Joseph will be her bridegroom forever, so she must put on her ancient, first wedding robe, her primordial garment (15:10). She offers the angel a meal of bread and wine (15:14), but the angel also wants a honeycomb. Since she has none, the angel miraculously supplies one made from the bees of Paradise who ate from the roses of Eden. It is the food of angels, and those who eat it never die (16:8). To prepare for the wedding, she puts on her first robe which shone like lightning (18:3), and on her glowing head she puts a golden wreath and a veil (18:5–6). They marry and live happily ever after—literally.

The element of the story most relevant to the present discussion, of course, is the angel's telling Asenath to remove her veil "because today you are a pure virgin and your head is like that of a young man." Several aspects of this trenchant statement merit comment. In the first place, earlier in the narrative we are told repeatedly that Asenath already was a virgin. Like many good maidens of *Märchen*, she is locked up in a tower and protected by a retinue of other virgins. In other words, she did not *become* a virgin when she met the angel, she had been one all along, and even as a virgin she wore her three protective head coverings. Furthermore, it is only in the presence of the angel that she removes her veil. When he leaves, she once again covers her head with a wreath and a veil. Her appearance as a young man is not permanent. Why? It would appear that the veil was inappropriate to her new status as one who, in ritual acts attended by an angel, had attained the primordial state.[111]

---

[111] It may be worth noting that in Philo's fascinating description of the Therapeutae in *De vita cont.* we are told these sectarians celebrated a meal after which the men and women would separate from each other, carry on like Maenads throughout the night by singing and dancing, and at dawn the two groups would merge with each other as the crowning moment. Philo's forced, rationalizing explanation helps little for understanding the function of this strange confluence of the sexes at dawn. Could this

To be sure, Asenath's act does not square precisely with the situation at Corinth. After performing these rites she marries Joseph and bears children. Notice, however, that Philo too, while considering marriage a divine gift, frequently spoke of women's transcending their femaleness and becoming like men. The point to be made here is simply that Asenath's ritual acts which returned her to the primordial condition, required her to remove her veil thus making her head like a man's.

I suggest these pneumatic Corinthian women in their ecstatic worship believed they too had climbed a rung on the ontological ladder, and transcended sexual differentiation.[112] To symbolize their new status, they removed their veils. Like Asenath, their heads for a time became "like that of a young man," like Eve's before her fall. Moreover, they too may well have removed veils at a holy meal. Paul had just completed a discussion of the Corinthians' claim to moral perfection by dint of having ingested "spiritual food" and "spiritual drink" (10:1–13), and of meals at which hosts offered meat offered to idols (10:14–11:2). Immediately after discussing veils Paul turns attention to abuses in Corinthian Eucharists (11:17–34). It is tempting—and in my view justified—to take all of 10:1–11:34 as a treatment of meals.

Becoming Male and Making the Two One

If correct, this hypothesis might seem to militate against our thesis that the Dominical Saying or its theological anthropology were present in Corinth. Becoming androgynous and women's imitating male appearance surely seem etymologically and logically contradictory, but not so for many ancients. For some of them, androgyny meant not bisexuality or asexuality but perfected masculinity. Wendy Doniger O'Flaherty's study of the androgyne image especially among Hindus helps us understand this apparent inconsistency:

> The androgyne may be primarily male—playing male social roles, having overwhelmingly male physical characteristics, man-

---

ecstatic moment have symbolized the reuniting of the sexes into the primordial androgyne?

[112] Robert Jewett ("Sexual Liberation of the Apostle Paul," 67) likewise states that Paul "appears to be arguing primarily against androgyny." See also Otto Bangerter, *Frauen im Aufbruch. Die Geschichte einer Frauenbewegung in der Alten Kirche. Ein Beitrag zur Frauenfrage* (Neukirchen-Vluyn: Neukirchener Verlag, 1971) 34–35.

ifesting male sexual patterns—and be regarded as highly positive by an androcentric society.[113]

The male androgyne is an example of the positive theology of the *coincidentia oppositorum* . . . the female androgyne is, however, generally regarded as a negative instance of *coincidentia oppositorum.*[114]

The notion that women must become male appears in Hellenistic Judaism, Valentinianism, and Syrian "Thomas" Christianity, the very circles identified with the Dominical Saying and its insistence that the two sexes become one. Philo states:

Progress is nothing else than the giving up of the female gender by changing into the male, since the female gender is material, passive, corporeal and sense-perceptible, while the male is active, rational, incorporeal and more akin to mind and thought.[115]

Passages like this can be found throughout Philo's writings.[116]

Although Valentinians claimed the sexes became one in the rite of the bridal chamber, they also insisted on destroying "the works of the female."[117] Clement of Alexandria accepted and Tertullian rejected this Valentinian paradox of uniting the sexes and making the female male. The first passage below is from Clement's *Stromateis,* the second from Tertullian's *Adv. Val.*

[To the true Gnostic] his wife after conception is as a sister . . . as being destined to become a sister in reality after putting off the flesh, which separates and limits the knowledge of those who are spiritual by the peculiar characteristics of the sexes. For souls themselves by themselves are equal. Souls are neither male nor female when they no longer marry nor are given in

[113] O'Flaherty, *Women, Androgynes, and Other Mythological Beasts* (Chicago: University of Chicago Press, 1980) 284.
[114] Ibid., 333.
[115] *Quest. Gen.* 1.8.
[116] See also *De vita cont.* 60–63; *De fuga* 128, 167; *De ebrietate* 59–61; *Quod det.* 28; *De post. Caini* 134; *De cherubim* 50–52; and *Quest. Exod.* 2.3.
[117] The *Gospel of the Egyptians* apud Clem. Al. *Strom.* 3.9.63; and the *Dial. Sav.* (NHC 3, 5) 138.15–20; 144.15–145.5.

marriage. And is not the woman translated into a man when
she is become equally unfeminine, and manly and perfect?[118]

I am still a man of the demiurge. I must turn aside where, after
the departure [death] there is no more giving in marriage, when
I have to put on in addition rather than be stripped, where even
if stripped, cut off from my sexuality, like the angels, neither
male nor female angel, no one will do anything against me, nor
will they find (me) a male.[119]

By removing from these passages the obviously polemical alterations
of the tradition,[120] one discovers that Valentinians claimed already to
have taken off the flesh and to have returned to a state of sexual
unity. Since souls are neither male nor female, they can no longer
marry nor be given in marriage. This sexual unity is not true androgyny but reconstituted masculinity, for the female must become
male.[121]

Likewise in the Syrian *Gospel of Thomas*, in spite of Jesus'
repeated command that the two sexes become one, he also says that
in order to retain Mary in the ranks of the disciples he "will make
her male, that she too may become a living spirit, resembling you
males. For every woman who makes herself male will enter the
Kingdom of Heaven" (logion 114). Notice too that in Gal 3:28 Paul
claims that believers are no longer male or female inasmuch as they
have become one male person ($\epsilon\hat{\iota}\varsigma$).

Instead of dismissing these examples either as unassimilated
conflations of conflicting traditions or as undisciplined speculation, I
would argue that the cause of this apparent inconsistency was a consistent exegesis of Genesis 1–3. The primordial unity was disrupted
by the creation and fall of the woman. Therefore, a return to that
unity necessitates an undoing of "the works of the female." As the
Gospel of Philip puts it: "If the woman had not separated from the

---

[118] Clem. Al. *Strom.* 6.12.100.

[119] Tert. *Adv. Val.* 32, 5.

[120] Of the two, Clement's version is closest to the original. He seems only to object
to the idea that one removes the body before death. Tertullian denounces the tradition at almost every point: he has not yet escaped the material world; he has not and
will not remove the flesh; and the ideal state of the soul is not masculinity but asexuality.

[121] According to Naassenes, Attis had achieved the ideal state of being "male-
female" ($\dot{\alpha}\rho\sigma\epsilon\nu\dot{o}\theta\eta\lambda\upsilon\varsigma$), but the elect must become wholly male (Hippol. *Haer.*
5.7.15, 5.8.44).

man, she would not die with the man."[122] If she joins with him again, giving up her femaleness, primordial unity is restored. Contrary to the opinion of many interpreters, the androgyne myth is not antiquity's answer to androcentrism; it is but one manifestation of it. We can even be more precise concerning the role of the Dominical Saying at Corinth. In one version of the saying the gender of Jesus' interlocutor is unclear, but in the other two his interlocutor is a woman (Salome in the *Gospel of the Egyptians*; Mary in the *Gospel of Thomas*). In other words, the tradition apparently understood the saying to pertain primarily to women. Furthermore, the Corinthian veils certainly could be understood as "garments of shame," symbols of ontological inferiority and subordination. If this were indeed the case, Paul's uses of "shame" ($\kappa\alpha\tau\alpha\iota\sigma\chi\acute{u}\nu\omega$, $\alpha\iota\sigma\chi\rho\acute{o}\varsigma$) in vss 4–6, "dishonor" ($\dot{\alpha}\tau\iota\mu\acute{\iota}\alpha$) in vs 14, and "glory" ($\delta\acute{o}\xi\alpha$) in vss 7–15 might be significant. Paul could be arguing that the veil is not a garment of shame but a garment of glory and authority.

To be sure, relating the Dominical Saying directly to the removal of veils at Corinth is speculative at best. Furthermore, it requires one to suppose that the saying had two interpretations: (1) the garment of shame was the prebaptismal garment symbolizing the body, and (2) the garment of shame was the veil removed at worship symbolizing the restoration of the androgny.

However, the *Acts of Thomas* tells a story in which the veil itself in one recension is called "the garment of shame." The parents of a virgin come to visit her the morning after her wedding. The couple, however, had not consummated their bond, but had converted to Thomas's ascetic gospel and were sitting opposite each other. The girl's head is unveiled. The exchange between parents and daughter may provide the best background of all on 1 Cor 11:3–16. The mother states:

> "Why dost thou sit thus, child, and art not ashamed, but dost behave as if thou hadst lived a long time with thine own husband?" And her father said: "Because of thy great love for thy husband dost thou not even veil thyself?"
>
> The bride in answer said: "Truly, father, I am in great love, and I pray to my Lord that the love which I experienced this night may remain with me, and I will ask for the husband of whom I have learned today. But that I do not veil myself is because the veil of shame [$\tau\grave{o}$ $\check{\epsilon}\sigma o\pi\tau\rho o\nu$ $\tau\hat{\eta}\varsigma$ $\alpha\iota\sigma\chi\acute{u}\nu\eta\varsigma$—the shorter

---

[122] (NHC 2, 3) 70.9–11.

recension reads τὸ ἔνδυμα τῆς αἰσχύνης: garment of shame] is taken from me; and I am no longer ashamed or abashed, because the work of shame and bashfulness has been removed far from me." [123]

Even if the Dominical Saying itself did not motivate the removal of Corinthian veils, its implied anthropology and interpretation of Genesis 1–3 most likely did. By reading 1 Cor 11:2–16 as a response to women's becoming like men, one can better untie the knotty questions mentioned at the outset.

Paul's Response to Women Looking Like Men

As we have seen, the Corinthians had an order of creation which informed their denial of a bodily resurrection (15:45–49). Their order seems to have been (1) God, (2) the incorporeal, sexually united Adam in the image of God, and (3) the corporeal, second Adam, from whom (4) the woman was formed. For Paul, on the other hand, the *ordo creationis* was (1) God, (2) Christ, (3) Adam, and (4) Eve. Not only is Paul's ordering different, its function is different too. The pneumatics apparently used theirs to encourage a return to the state of the spiritual Adam. Paul uses his to sanction as divine—and therefore natural—the ontological inferiority of women.

Pneumatics	1 Cor 11:3 and 7–9
God	God ("head" of Christ)
(Wisdom) [124]	Christ (omitted in 7–9) ("head" of a man)
spiritual Adam (image of God)	
material Adam	man ("image" and "glory" of God; "head" of a woman)
woman	woman ("glory" of a man)

In spite of these differences, however, there also are similarities. Both place women at the bottom of the ladder, and —if we take Philo's discussion of the order that appears in the lefthand

---

[123] *Acts Thom.* 13–14.

[124] Senft (*La première épître*, 141) rightly points out that in 1 Cor 11:3 Paul has placed Christ in the place usually given wisdom. See also Jervell, *Imago Dei*, 259.

column—both express the relationship of one rung to the next as type/copy. When Philo speaks of types he uses "paradigm" (παράδειγμα),[125] "archetype" (ἀρχέτυπον),[126] "seal" (σφραγίς),[127] "idea" (ἰδέα),[128] "genus" (γένος),[129] "origin" (ἀρχή),[130] and "stamp" (χαρακτήρ).[131] To speak of copies he uses "copy" (μίμημα),[132] "impress" (ἐκμαγεῖον),[133] "coin" (νόμισμα),[134] "effulgence" (ἀπαύγασμα),[135] "replica" (τύπος),[136] "representation" (ἀπεικόνισμα),[137] and "image" (εἰκών).[138] To express copy Paul uses "image" (εἰκών) and "glory" (δόξα). If "image" and "glory" are more or less synonyms, we must assume that Paul denied women were fully in the divine image.[139] To express "type"

---

[125] Leg. all. 3.96; De op. mun. 130; Quis her. 231; De conf. 63; Quod det. 87.

[126] Leg. all. 1.43; 2.4; Quis her. 126, 230; Quod det. 78, 86; De spec. leg. 3.83.

[127] De op. mun. 25; 129; 134; Quod det. 86; De plant. 18.

[128] Leg. all. 1.21–22, 33, 42; 2.12; De op. mun. 129, 134; Quod det. 78.

[129] Leg. all. 2.13; De op. mun. 134; Quod det. 78; De mut. nom. 78–80.

[130] Leg. all. 1.43.

[131] Leg. all. 1.61; Quod det. 83; De plant. 18.

[132] Leg. all. 1.43; 2.4; De op. mun. 25; 139; Quis her. 126; 230; Quod det. 83.

[133] De op. mun. 146; Quis her. 231; De spec. leg. 3.83; De mut. nom. 223.

[134] De plant. 18.

[135] De op. mun. 146; De spec. leg. 4.123.

[136] Leg. all. 1.61; Quod det. 78, 83, 86.

[137] Leg. all. 3.96; Quis her. 231; Quod det. 83; De plant. 20.

[138] Leg. all. 1.31, 33; 3.96; De op. mun. 25; Quis her. 231; Quod det. 82; 86; De spec. leg. 1.81; 3.83; De mut. nom. 223.

[139] Notice how εἰκών and δόξα function together in 2 Cor 3:18–4:6. See Friedrich-Wilhelm Eltester, Eikon im Neuen Testament (BZNW 23; Berlin: Töpelmann, 1958) 155–56; Jervell, Imago Dei, 296–301; and Edvin Larsson, Christus als Vorbild. Eine Untersuchung zu den paulinischen Tauf- und Eikontexten (ASNU 23; Uppsala: Gleerup and Munksgaard, 1962) 183–87; Gerhard Kittel, "εἰκών," TDNT 2 (1964) 394–95. In Num. Rab. 3:8 the glory of God relates only to men.

For references to Adam's glory and his losing it see CD 3.20; 1QS 4.23; 2 Bar. 15:8; 51; 54:15–21; Apoc. Moses 20:1–2; 21:6; and 39:2.

At first sight, this denial of the divine image to the woman appears to be a blatant perversion of Gen 1:26 27; but in a detailed study of speculations on the image of God in postbiblical Judaism, Gnosticism, and Paul, Jacob Jervell (Imago Dei, 298–303) has shown how Paul might have interpreted Gen 1–2 and 5:1–5. Gen 1:27 and 5:1–2 read as follows:

> God created the human in His image. In the image of God he created him. Male and female He created them. (1:27)

> God created Adam; in the likeness of God He created him. Male and female He created them. (5:1–2)

In both cases, the image of God is related to the singular pronoun, never to the plural. This is even more pronounced in Greek. The LXX, by translating the

Paul uses "head" (κεφαλή), perhaps because it is a more personal, organic, and intimate term than those used generally in Hellenistic Judaism, or—more likely—because it allows the word play on "head" in vss 4–5.[140]

In this connection it is interesting to note that in 2 Corinthians Paul again relates the divine image and its glory to the head and face. Moses veiled his face because his glory was so dazzling (2 Cor 3:7–11) and because he wanted to conceal its diminishment (vss 12–16). However, such veils were unnecessary for believers in Christ.

> And we all, with unveiled face, beholding the glory of the Lord, are being changed into his likeness from one degree of glory to another. (3:18)

> In their case the god of this world has blinded the minds of the unbelievers, to keep them from seeing the light of the gospel of the glory of Christ, who is the likeness of God. (4:4)

> For it is the God who said, "Let light shine out of darkness," who has shone in our hearts to give the light of the knowledge of the glory of God in the face of Christ. (4:6)

In 11:2–16 Paul objects that the undifferentiated appearance of men and women prophesying violates natural order and dishonors the woman's "head," that is, her husband, by breaking with socially approved fashions.[141] The veil is not the result of a curse on Eve, but is required by God's very act of creation. Furthermore, a woman cannot symbolize authority by removing her veil, because the veil itself is an authority over the angels. A man, on the other hand, because he is more fully participant in the image of God, dishonors

---

anarthrous ʾādām in 5:1 with the name Adam, implies that only he was in God's image. Philo too divided 1:27b, "in the image of God He created him," which speaks of the unified human in God's image, from 1:27c, "male and female He created them," which speaks of the sexually divided one. " 'Male and female He made'—not now 'him' but 'them' " (*Quis her.* 164). The *Pseudo-Clementines* alter the "them" in Gen 1:27c to "him": "male and female He created *him*" (*Hom.* 3.54.2). The Rabbis knew a version of the Septuagint with a similar reading (*b. Meg.* 9a and *Mek.*, Pisḥa 14). See also *b.* ʿ*Erubin* 18a.

[140] See Heinrich Schlier, "κεφαλή," *TDNT* 3 (1965) 673–82: "κεφαλή implies one who stands over another in the sense of being the ground of his being. Paul could have used ἀρχή if there had not been a closer personal relationsip in κεφαλή" (p. 679). See also Clem. Al. *Exc. Theod.* 33.2; and Iren. *Adv. haer.* 1.5.3.

[141] For a parallel argument from nature regarding sexual distinction related to hair see Epictetus 1.16.10.

Christ, his metaphorical head, if he covers his head. By so doing he denies the authority of God's image. We need not suppose with Tertullian and a host of subsequent interpreters that the angels in question were demonic, like the "Watchers" of Gen 6:1–4. Paul considered all angels ambiguous and potentially dangerous powers.[142] It remains unclear, however, what Paul understood as the source of the veil's authority. Perhaps Paul meant that the veil, as a sign of marital subordination, represents the authority of a husband (cf. 1 Cor 7:4: "A woman does not have authority over [ἐξουσιάζει] her own body, but the man does."), in which case the veil would not apply to unmarried women.[143] Such a distinction between married and unmarried women, however, is otherwise lacking in the passage. Moreover, such metonymic uses of ἐξουσία are unknown.

It is more likely that Paul had in mind some active meaning. He probably considered the veil an apotropaic talisman, like a charm against curses or an amulet against the evil eye. Martin Dibelius has collected several parallels from ancient sources illustrating the assumed magical powers of head coverings.[144] Perhaps Paul feared that in ecstasy women were especially vulnerable to spirits. It is also possible that Paul identified authority with a veil because of an Aramaic folk etymology that related the root *šlṭ*, "authority" with a common word for veil, *šilṭônayāh*.[145]

It might be possible now to provide an interpretive paraphrase in outline for the entire passage.

Captatio Benevolentiae (vs 2)

> I praise you for remembering
> me in all respects and for
> maintaining the traditions as
> I passed them on to you.

---

[142] Alan Richardson claims: "There are no good angels in St Paul" (*An Introduction to the Theology of the New Testament* [New York: Harper, 1958] 209). See also Gerhard Kittel, "ἄγγελος," *TDNT* 1 (1964) 85–86; and Hurd, *Origin of I Corinthians*, 184, n. 4.

[143] For evidence of the veil as a symbol of authority over the woman see Str-B 3. 435–39.

[144] Dibelius, *Geisterwelt*, 19–20. See Homer *Odyssey* 312–80 where Ino's veil protects Odysseus from Poseidon.

[145] See above n. 33.

I. An Appeal to the Order of Creation (vss 3–12)

    A. Hierarchy of Creation (vs 3)

> But I want you to know that your order of crea-
> tion is wrong—namely, that God's image was
> the pattern for the first Adam, who therefore
> was immaterial and sexualy undivided, and that
> this first Adam was the pattern for the second,
> the material Adam, who was subsequently
> divided into genders. Rather, God is the head
> (immediate ontological source and authority) of
> Christ

and Christ is the head
of every man

                    and the man is the head
                    of every woman.

    B. Hierarchy Applied to Worship (vss 4–6)

Every man who prays or proph-
esies with his head veiled
shames Christ, his head, inasmuch as he thereby denies the
power of God's image which he
bears.

                    And every woman who prays or
                    prophesies with her head unveiled
                    shames her husband, her head, by
                    removing her symbol of subjec-
                    tion, by usurping his prerogative,
                    and by breaking with recognized
                    social conventions. She is no
                    different from a woman who has
                    had her head shaved. For if a
                    woman removes her veil, she
                    might as well shave off her hair.
                    If it is disgraceful for a woman to
                    be shorn or shaved—as is most
                    surely the case—it is disgraceful
                    also for her to be unveiled.

C. The Application Defended (vss 7-10)

For a man ought not be veiled, for according to Gen 1:27 he is the image and glory of God. "In the image of God he made him."

But the woman is the image and glory of the man.

For man is not from woman, And man was not created for the sake of the woman,

but woman from man.

but, according to Gen 2:8-15, the woman for the sake of the man. Because the woman is not directly in God's image, and therefore does not enjoy its authority, the veil becomes for her a kind of ersatz authority, which she needs to wear because of her vulnerability to the spirit world when she engages in ecstatic worship. So, you see, she symbolizes her participation in the authority of the divine image not by removing her veil, as you had supposed, but by wearing it.

D. The Hierarchy Qualified (vss 11-12)

However, in the Christian community

woman cannot exist without man

nor man exist without woman.

For as a woman came from a man in the sequence of creation,

a man comes into being through a woman's childbearing.

And of course all things ultimately come from God.

II. Appeal to Nature and Convention (vss 13–15)

> Judge for yourselves.
>> Is it appropriate for a woman to pray to God unveiled?

> Does not nature herself teach us that

if a man wears long hair it
dishonors him,

>> and if a woman wears long hair it is her glory? Long hair has been given her as a kind of garment.

III. An Appeal to Christian Custom (vs 16)

>> If someone still wants to argue about this, that one must realize that no other Christian community allows women to pray or prophesy unveiled.

Women's Liberation at Corinth

In spite of the obvious sexism implicit in the notion that women must become male, we should acknowledge the emancipating emotional release women experienced in ecstatic removal of their symbols of subordination. Female worshippers in Greco-Roman religions frequently removed their veils and let down their hair.[146] The watershed in Asenath's legendary development from a cloistered virgin under her father's rule to a Hebrew matriarch was her cultic unveiling. Thecla, the archetypal liberated Christian woman in the *Acts of Paul,* symbolized her freedom by cutting her hair short and wearing men's clothing.[147] One night, Perpetua dreamed she was about to fight the devil and saw herself stripped naked for the contest and transformed into a man.[148] Jerome complains that some ascetic women "change their garb and assume the mien of men,

---

[146] See Van Unnik, "Les cheveux défaits," 87–89; R. and C. Kroeger, "Inquiry into Evidence of Maenadism," 331–35; and Schüssler Fiorenza, *In Memory of Her,* 227–28.

[147] *Acts Paul* 3.25, 40. For the significance of Thecla in the early church see my book, *The Legend and the Apostle: The Battle for Paul in Story and Canon* (Philadelphia: Westminster, 1983).

[148] *Martyrdom of Perpetua and Felicitas* 10.7.

being ashamed of being what they were born to be—women. They cut off their hair and are not ashamed to look like Eunuchs."[149] The Council of Gangra (fourth century) legislated against women donning men's clothing when they take vows of chastity. Only if the practice had been widespread would it have merited such official denunciation.

> If a woman, under pretence of leading an ascetic life, change her apparel, and instead of the accustomed habit of women take that of men, let her be anathema.[150]

No matter how strange this religiously motivated transvestism may appear to us, for these women wearing men's clothing surely was a sign of their liberation.[151]

However, we must not view Paul's opposition to cultic transvestism in Corinth simply as a sexist reaction to woman's liberation. For him, women's freedom consists not in their becoming like men in cultic transcendence of the soul but in their indispensibility *as women* in procreation and "in the Lord," that is, in the Christian community (1 Cor 11:11–12).

In this respect, most feminists would agree more with Paul than with the Corinthians. Behind much of the misogyny of western cultures is the Platonic devaluation of the body and the attending male contemptuous fascination with the female anatomy. Consequently, women rightly have seen that their liberation in part requires a transvaluation of embodiment and especially of women's anatomical functions. "Our Bodies Ourselves" is more than the title of a popular book; it is a celebrative expression of corporeality. Modern feminists, therefore, would side with Corinthian women in their removal of tokens of ontic inferiority, but with Paul in his rejection of disembodiment and becoming male as soteriological goals.

It would be naive for us simply to decide whether the Corinthians or Paul were more liberated. The issues historically and theoretically are far too complex to permit such a facile choice. On the one hand, one could argue that both the Corinthians and Paul elevated women in the community to a status higher than in society at large. Women

---

[149] Letter 22, *To Eustochium* 27.

[150] Crawley, *Dress, Drinks, and Drums*, 154.

[151] On celibacy and women's liberation see Rosemary Radford Ruether, "Mothers of the Church: Ascetic Women in the Late Patristic Age," in idem and Eleanor McLaughlin, eds., *Women of Spirit: Female Leadership in the Jewish and Christian Traditions* (New York: Simon & Schuster, 1979) 71–98.

as well as men could pray, prophesy, and speak in tongues. According to the Corinthians, women could transcend their ontic inferiority in ecstacy; according to Paul, women's roles in procreation and community qualified their subordination to men (11:11–12). On the other hand, neither party sufficiently challenged patriarchalism. To be sure, Corinthian women experienced freedom in removing their veils, but at the price of their identities as women. Paul may have desired men and women to become one in the community, but he insisted on the derivative and subordinate status of women implied by his understanding of Genesis. It would therefore appear that 1 Cor 11:2–16 relates to modern struggles for sexual equality only obliquely. It is our task not to choose sides, but to inquire of ourselves how the oppressive status given women in most human societies might be transformed by the gospel.

Conclusion

The theology of the Dominical Saying characterizes the "pneumatics" at Corinth who had been influenced, presumably through the teaching of Apollos, by Philonic exegesis on Genesis. This theology included the flight of the soul from the body before death, baptismal perfectionism, and celibacy mandated by ascetic sayings of Jesus.

Surely it is significant that we find Paul addressing these theologoumena almost exclusively in his correspondence with Corinth. Paul used garment imagery in polemics over anthropology only when writing to Corinth,[152] opposed sacramental perfectionism only in 1 Corinthians,[153] and opposed those who claimed already to have achieved the resurrection only once outside of the Corinthian correspondence (Phil 3:9–21). Paul spoke against obligatory celibacy only in 1 Corinthians. Women removed their head coverings only in Corinth. There is evidence only from Corinth that Jesus traditions informed sexual practice. Outside of 1 Corinthians Paul argues theologically from Genesis only in Rom 5:12–13, which was written *from* Corinth. But in 1 Corinthians Paul argues from Genesis no less than four times, and in the very contexts relevant to the Dominical Saying: the resurrection of the body (1 Cor 15:22, 45–49), sexual practices (1 Cor 6:16–17), and distinctions between the sexes (1 Cor 11:3–10). Furthermore, it is possible the

---

[152] 1 Cor 15:45–49, 53–54; 2 Cor 5:2–5.
[153] 1 Cor 10:1–12; 11:17–34; and perhaps 1:16–22 and 3:21–4:7.

Corinthian women removed their veils as so many "garments of shame" thereby expressing their regained authority in God's image, which is "neither male nor female." Paul, on the other hand, claimed veils were garments of honor, symbols of authority over the angels who view the worship of both males and females—most appropriately dressed as males and females. As we shall see, Paul's arguments with the Corinthians on these matters correspond with his alteration of the Dominical Saying in Gal 3:26–28.

4

THE DOMINICAL SAYING
AND GALATIANS 3:26–28

To this point we have seen that the Dominical Saying and Gal 3:26–28 share striking formal and thematic features (Chapter 1), that the saying plays on a distinctive baptismal anthropology (Chapter 2), and that this anthropology characterized the pneumatics at Corinth (Chapter 3). In this chapter we shall compare the Dominical Saying and Gal 3:26–28 in more detail in order better to delineate the genetic linkages between them.

From the outset we must recognize that the plasticity of oral/aural communication makes ambiguous any hypothetical rectilinear line of development. Oral traditions are protean not geometric. For example, if one were to agree with the consensus that Gal 3:26–28, 1 Cor 12:13, and Col 3:9–11 all cite a common oral baptismal saying, the radical variations among these three versions demonstrate its elasticity. Were one to claim—as I shall—that the Dominical Saying better represents the tradition behind Gal 3:26–28 than Gal 3:26–28 itself, the variations in the *Gospel of the Egyptians*, *2 Clement*, and the *Gospel of Thomas* likewise show how malleable the saying was. Therefore, we must abandon any attempt to isolate an *Urform*, a prototype or paradigm from which one could deduce the variations.

At times in this chapter the reader may sense that I violate my own caveats by comparing the Dominical Saying and Gal 3:26–28 too woodenly. Unfortunately, there is no alternative apart from despairing of the enterprise altogether. One cannot take a tape recorder to ancient Achaea or Galatia to study these baptismal utterances with the sophistication of a modern folklorist. One can monitor the flow of this undulating stream of oral performances only by analyzing the few textually frozen chunks that have come down to us. My hope throughout is that a careful comparison of these chunks will allow us to determine whether the source of that stream is better characterized by the sayings in the *Gospel of the Egyptians*, *2 Clement*, and the *Gospel of Thomas*, or by those in Gal 3:26–28, 1 Cor 12:13, and Col 3:9–11.

4.1 Which Is More Primitive?

In favor of giving priority to Gal 3:26–28 and parallels is the relative anteriority of Galatians itself, written decades before the earliest witness to the Dominical Saying. For most interpreters this consideration settles the matter. Robert M. Grant, Wayne A. Meeks, Hartwig Thyen, Hans Dieter Betz, Henning Paulsen, and Bernard H. Brinsmead see in the Dominical Saying evidence that Christian Gnostics employed the androgyne myth—potentially if not actually present in Gal 3:26–28—to express transformations of subjective consciousness or of sexual interrelationships.[1] They assume that both Gal 3:26–28 and the saying derive from a common source, though the version in Galatians has preserved its earliest discernible form. Marie de Merode thinks the Dominical Saying shows how some Christians of the second century distorted Gal 3:28 in order to justify their denunciations of marriage.[2] Unfortunately, these scholars do not bolster their theories with detailed form-critical analyses. Neither does Schüssler Fiorenza, though she differs from these interpreters by claiming that the Dominical Saying originally is not Gnostic but "reflects the same community situation as Gal 3:28,"[3] that is, that "women and men in the Christian community are not defined by their sexual procreative capacities . . . but by their discipleship

---

[1] Grant, *The Secret Sayings of Jesus* (New York: Doubleday: 1960) 144; Meeks, "Image of the Androgyne," 193–97; Thyen, "'. . . nicht mehr mannlich und weiblich . . .,'" 140–41; Betz, *Galatians*, 195–96; Paulsen, "Einheit und Freiheit," 80–84; Brinsmead, *Galatians—Dialogical Response to Opponents*, 148–56. This seems to be the position also of H. E. W. Turner, "The Theology of the Gospel of Thomas," in idem and Hugh Montefiore, eds., *Thomas and the Evangelists* (SBT; Naperville: Allenson, 1962) 103; K. O. Schmidt, *Die geheimen Herren-Worte des Thomas-Evangeliums. Wegweisungen Christi zur Selbstvollendung* (Pfullingen/Württ.: Baum-Verlag, 1966) 83; and Jacques-É. Ménard, *L'évangile selon Thomas*, 113.

[2] Merode, "Théologie primitive de la femme?," 188.

[3] Schüssler Fiorenza, *In Memory of Her*, 212.

and empowering with the Spirit.''[4] Kurt Niederwimmer and Gerhard Dautzenberg provide the only detailed discussions of the formal similarities between the Dominical Saying and Gal 3:26–28.

Niederwimmer traces both back to "a saying from primitive Christian enthusiasm" which declared sexual distinctions already passé and legitimated libertine sexual practices. Gal 3:28 preserves the earliest form of the saying inasmuch as it retains the present tense ("There is no . . ."). The preacher of *2 Clement* makes the saying eschatological ("When you have done these things . . .") in order to dodge its revolutionary implications. The *Gospel of the Egyptians* and the *Gospel of Thomas* "gnosticize" it and enlist it for the cause of celibacy.[5]

Dautzenberg doubts Gal 3:26–28 ever was a pre-Pauline formula. The tradition behind the text is not a verbal formula but the actual experience of emancipation from social distinctions in Pauline churches. Paul reminds the Galatians (and the Corinthians in 1 Cor 12:13) of this freedom; later, Gnostics transformed this Pauline reminder into an eschatological projection shaped by speculations that the soul's ultimate state would be a "new creation" as expressed in Col 3:10–11. It was only natural, then, that the social pairs of Galatians became anthropological (inside/outside, male/female) and cosmic (above/below, right/left).[6]

However, when one disregards the anteriority of Galatians, other considerations suggest the direction of dependence flowed in the opposite direction. For example, it is clear that early Christians transmitted the Dominical Saying orally. We may safely disallow any literary interrelationship between the *Gospel of the Egyptians, 2 Clement,* and the *Gospel of Thomas.* The author of each apparently received the saying independently from oral tradition, and each treated it as an authentically dominical pronouncement. Furthermore, by the middle of the second century the saying emerged in communities with widely divergent theologies and in widely scattered areas: Egypt (the *Gospel of the Egyptians*), Greece (*2 Clement*), and Syria (the *Gospel of Thomas*). Even Clement of Alexandria found it necessary to give his own pious interpretation of it.[7]

[4] Ibid., 212–13.
[5] Niederwimmer, *Askese und Mysterium,* 177–79.
[6] Dautzenberg, " 'Da ist nicht männlich und weiblich,' " 190–91.
[7] *Strom.* 3.13.93.

On the other hand, it is far more difficult to demonstrate that early Christians ever orally transmitted a saying equivalent to that usually reconstituted from Gal 3:26–28 and parallels. In the case of Col 3:9–11 one might reasonably argue that the deutero-Pauline author, who apparently knew Galatians, was merely revising Gal 3:26–28 for his own purposes, and not citing oral tradition at all.

With respect to 1 Cor 12:13 it is interesting to note that here we no longer find the indicators that Paul was dependent on oral tradition in Gal 3:26–28, that is, the change of person from "we" to "you," the reference to putting on Christ, the chiasm among the pairs of opposites, and the reference to "male and female." Furthermore, absent in 1 Cor 12:13 are the features that made Gal 3:26–28 and the Dominical Saying most similar. Said otherwise, 1 Cor 12:13 has in common with Gal 3:26–28 precisely what Gal 3:26–28 does not have in common with the Dominical Saying.

Dom. Saying	Gal 3:26–28	1 Cor 12:13
(2d p. pl.)	(2d p. pl.)	(1st p. pl.)
	baptized into Christ	baptized into one body
garment	put on Christ	
two become one	Jew/Greek	Jews/Greeks
	slave/free	slaves/free
male/female	male/female	
	all are one in Christ	all have drunk of one spirit.

It would appear that the parallel in 1 Corinthians does not reflect a traditional saying at all but Paul's own convictions about the social unification implied by Christian rituals. One might even use 1 Cor 12:13 to isolate Paul's redactional alterations of the Dominical Saying in Gal 3:26–28 inasmuch as in 1 Corinthians, as in Galatians, the issue is Jew/Greek and slave/free.

Notice also that the Dominical Saying and Gal 3:26–28 use the negative phrases "neither . . . nor," or "there is no . . . or . . ." while 1 Corinthians uses the positive "either . . . or." This difference is significant. In 1 Cor 12:13 the emphasis is no longer on the abolition of social differences but the integration of these different groups into one body. *Vive la différence* in 1 Corinthians; *détruise la différence* in Galatians. Inasmuch as the abolition of social distinctions appears only when Paul interprets the Dominical Saying and its abolition of sexual distinctions, perhaps we should assume

that he never intended to deny the existence of social distinctions
but that he intended to celebrate them in the acceptance of all people
in the new creation.

From the foregoing one might reasonably assume that whereas the
Dominical Saying undeniably circulated orally, Gal 3:26–28 circulated only on papyrus. However, the most compelling reasons for
viewing the Dominical Saying as the more original saying issue from
comparing it theologically with Gal 3:26–28. I present the two sayings side-by-side once more to facilitate this comparison.

Dominical Saying	Gal 3:26–28
	For in Christ all of you are sons of God through faith, for as many of you as have been baptized into Christ
When you tread upon the garment of shame,	have put on Christ.
and when the two become one,	There is no Jew or Greek.
[and the outside as the inside]	There is no slave or free.
and the male with the female	
neither male nor female.	There is no male and female. For you all are one in Christ Jesus.

The rest of this chapter attempts to answer the following four
questions of these parallels:

1. Which is the more traditional: "tread on the garment of shame"
or "put on Christ"?
2. Which is the more traditional: "the two become one" or "all of
you are one"?
3. Which is the more traditional: the anthropological opposites (in-
side/outside, male/female) or the social opposites (Jew/Greek,
slave/free, male/female)?
4. Is it more likely that later tradition "eschatologized" Gal 3:28 or
that Paul "historicized" the Dominical Saying?

4.2 Putting on Christ

It is unlikely that that Gnostics would have transformed the phrase
"you have put on Christ" in Gal 3:27 to "when you tread on the

garment of shame." Valentinians, for example, had no objection whatever to the idea of putting on Christ; in fact, putting on Christ is made possible only by putting off the body.[8]

However, as we have seen, Paul debunked the idea of putting off the body as a "garment of shame." The body must not be put off; rather, it must put on incorruption (1 Cor 15:53–54), it must "put on in addition":

> Here indeed we groan, and long to put on our heavenly dwelling, so that by putting it on we may not be found naked. For while we are still in this tent, we sigh with anxiety; not that we would be unclothed [of the body], but that we would be further clothed so that what is mortal may be swallowed up by life. (2 Cor 5:2–4)[9]

---

[8] *Gos. Phil.* (NHC 2, 3) 75.21–24; *Tri. Trac.* (NHC 1, 5) 87.1–4. Cf. *Odes Sol.* 7:4; 31:12. This mutation in Pauline images whereby Paul's intention becomes inverted may be illustrated in the apparent docetic textual alterations of 2 Cor 5:2–4. Codex Bezae, a number of old Latin manuscripts, and the texts used by Marcion and Chrysostom read "put off" (ἐκδυσάμενοι) in 2 Cor 5:3 instead of "put on" (ἐνδυσάμενοι), thereby making the passage read like this:

> For in this (body or dwelling) indeed we groan, and desire to put on our heavenly dwelling. And even if we put off (the body) we will not be found naked. For indeed, while we are in this tent we groan because we are weighed down (with corporality), not because we want to be unclothed, but to be clothed.

This is the very anthropology Paul originally opposed in this passage.

A similar phenomenon can be seen in the textual witnesses to 1 Cor 15:49. "And as we have worn the image of the earthly (Adam), we also shall wear the image of the heavenly." But by far the majority of manuscripts, including the text used by Marcion and Theodotus the Valentinian read "Let us wear," not "We shall wear." Here again the tradition shows no reticence in speaking of putting on Christ. One should put on Christ *now* because one no longer wears the image of the earthly Adam. Paul is turned against Paul by the substitution of an omega for an omicron.

[9] Apart from Gal 3:27 Paul speaks of "putting on Christ" only in Rom 13:12–14, and here too he avoids joining it to putting off the flesh:

> The night is far gone, the day is at hand. Let us then cast off the works of darkness and put on the armor of light . . . but put on the Lord Jesus Christ, and make no provision for the flesh to gratify its desires.

The natural extension of the garment imagery and chiasmus would have been for Paul to have said at the end, "cast off the flesh," not "make no provision for the flesh." He avoided this chiasm: when one puts on Christ one does not put off the flesh, one controls it and puts off its works.

Paul's refusal to say the body must be put off conforms with his apparent alteration of the Dominical Saying: treading on the garment of shame becomes "putting on Christ."

4.3 All Become One

Whereas the Dominical Saying requires that "the two become one" (ἕν, neuter), Paul insists that in Christ "*all* are one" (εἷς, masculine). Deciding which of the two is the more original is difficult. Those giving priority to the latter usually argue that later tradition elaborated the traces of the myth of the primordial androgyne found already in Gal 3:28 or in the saying it reflects. Although this explanation is plausible, three observations make it more likely that Paul modulated the androgyne myth of the Dominical Saying into an affirmation of the unity of *all* in the community.

First, Paul seems to have been unsympathetic to the primordial androgyne myth. The *ordo creationis* in 1 Corinthians 11 precludes Adam's androgyny, and in 1 Cor 15:45–49 he refutes those who divided the Genesis creation accounts into two successive creations of Adam. Elsewhere when Paul speaks of the "new creation" he alludes not to the reunification of the sexes but of Jews and Greeks: "For neither circumcision counts for anything, nor uncircumcision, but a new creation" (Gal 6:15). According to Jacob Jervell, Paul refers to this unity as a new creation because Jews commonly thought Gentiles had not been created in the divine image.[10]

Derwood C. Smith has shown that the author of Ephesians, like Paul, employed the myth of the primordial androgyne to image the unity of Jews and Greeks.[11]

> For he himself is our peace, who *made both one* and destroyed the wall of partition . . . *in order that he might create in him the two into one new human* making peace, and in order to reconcile *both in one body* to God through the cross. . . . And he came and preached peace to you who were far off and peace to those who

---

[10] Jervell states: "We now know from the debates concerning the divine image in late Judaism that it correlates with the concept of Israel's own divine image. The gentile simply does not bear the divine image. As the Law then had been decisive for the possession of the divine image, here it is in Christ. As Israel was considered the creation, here it is the Christian community" (*Imago Dei*, 251).

[11] Smith, "The Two Made One: Some Observations on Ephesians 2:14–18," *Ohio Journal of Religious Studies* (1973) 34–54.

were near; for through him *we both, in one spirit* have access to the Father. (Eph 2:14–18)

Surely Paul would have been delighted to learn that this pseudo-Paul so admirably expressed his own position.

Second, had Gnostics later reshaped Gal 3:28 into the Dominical Saying, it is unclear why they would have changed the masculine gender for the word "one" (εἷς) to the neuter (ἕν). As we have seen, androgyny in such traditions functioned as a return to reconstituted masculinity, the woman becoming male. It is easier to explain this disagreement in gender for the word "one" in the two passages by supposing that Paul made the neuter masculine. Why? Because the new, reunified creation is none other than Christ himself.

Third, Paul would not have tolerated any view of baptism that threatened to undermine the unity of the community, as is apparent from his opposition to the divisiveness of baptism at Corinth. Paul learned from "Chloe's people" that the community had splintered into several factions each claiming the authority of an apostle: "I am of Paul . . . Apollos . . . or Cephas."[12] By disclaiming his own role as a baptizer (1:13–17), Paul implies that baptism into an apostle's name or by an apostle had fostered partisanship. Insofar as baptism symbolized for them an individual's flight from the world, the Corinthians did not consider these divisions a violation of the rite. Paul did. For him, baptism was a rite not of individual transcendence but of social unification, of membership in Christ's body, the community. All become one. In his denunciation of the division caused by "spiritual gifts" Paul introduces his understanding of baptism as the great equalizer.

> For just as the body is one and has many members, and all the members of the body, though many, are one body, so it is with Christ. For by one Spirit we were all baptized into one body— Jews and Greeks, slaves or free—and all were made to drink of one spirit. (12:12–13)

In Galatians he opposed another kind of division, that between Jews and Greeks, and in his appropriation of the Dominical Saying he again used body imagery to depict the social unity symbolized by baptism:

---

[12] 1 Cor 1:10–12; cf. 3:4, 22.

For *in Christ Jesus* you are all sons of God . . .

For as many of you as were baptized *into Christ* have *put on Christ* . . .

For you are all one *in Christ Jesus.* (Gal 3:27–28)

Paul's use of the phrase "in Christ" almost always is spatial, and it is here as well. "Christ is the 'place' in whom believers are and in whom salvation is."[13] Also spatial is the image of putting on Christ: initiates have become part of Christ's body. The same interpretation is justified in the case of "baptized into Christ."[14]

It would therefore appear likely that Paul transformed the individualistic, sexual unity expressed in the Dominical Saying into social unity. This transformation corresponds with his statements in 1 Corinthians insisting that baptism, as a rite of unification, is violated by social fission.

4.4 Jew/Greek, Slave/Free, Male/Female

Did later tradition transform Paul's list of social opposites into anthropological opposites or did Paul transform the anthropological opposites into social opposites? First, we should observe that Gnostics had no objection to celebrating the unification of social opposites in the community. One can see this in the following passage from the Valentinian *Tripartite Tractate*:

For when we confessed the Kingdom which is in Christ, we escaped from the whole multiplicity of forms and from inequality and change. For the end will receive a unitary existence just as the beginning, where there is no male nor female, nor slave and free, nor circumcision and uncircumcision, neither angel nor man, but Christ is all in all. ([NHC 1, 5] 132.16–28)

---

[13] Ernest Best, *One Body in Christ: A Study in the Relationship of the Church to Christ in the Epistles of the Apostle Paul* (London: SPCK, 1955) 7–8.

[14] Some scholars have taken this phrase as a shortened form of being baptized into the *name* of Christ (e.g., George Beasely-Murray, *Baptism in the New Testament* [London: Macmillan, 1962] 129), but Paul never directly used "baptized into the name," even though he knew of it and apparently approved of it (1 Cor 1:13, 15). But Best concludes that "there is no argument . . . sufficiently strong to force us to alter our conclusion that in the phrase βαπτίζειν εἰς Χριστόν, εἰς is to be given a 'local' or 'spatial' connotation" (*One Body*, 73).

Carpocratians considered all people equal: "There is no distinction between rich and poor, people and governor, stupid and clever, female and male, free men and slaves."[15] In the *Acts of Thomas* Mygdonia longs for heaven, "where there is neither day and night, nor light and darkness, nor good and evil, nor poor and rich, male and female, no free and slave, no proud that subdues the humble."[16]

But whereas Gnostics did not object to a program of social unification, Paul objected to the Corinthians' anthropological reform, that is, their putative release from the body and return to androgyny. "Neither male nor female" would have been acceptable to Paul only if it meant the overcoming of sexual distinctions and antagonisms between men and women in the community.

Why did Paul select these three pairs of opposites to express this social unity? If Paul were in fact interpreting the Dominical Saying, one might simply say he saw in the male/female pair a reference to social unity from which he generated the pairs Jew/Greek and slave/free.[17] S. Scott Bartchy suggests that these three pairs are linked "in a thought-pattern which represented *Paul's* understanding of the 'break-through' in Christ."[18] This "thought-pattern," Bartchy argues, lies behind 1 Cor 7:17–28 where Paul discusses these social divisions in precisely the same order: circumcision/uncircumcision in vss 17–28; slave/free in vss 21–24; and men/women in vss 25–28. Furthermore, there can be little doubt that each of these three pairs represents actual social challenges to Paul's mission. Had he indeed known the Dominical Saying and had he wanted to alter it to express social reunification, these are precisely the pairs of opposites we would have expected him to use.

Similar pairs of opposites are found also in a well-known Hellenistic thanksgiving variously attributed to Thales and Plato.[19] The philosopher gives thanks first, ". . . that I was born a human being and not one of the brutes; next, that I was born a man and not a woman;

---

[15] Clem. Al. *Strom.* 3.2.6 (the translation comes from John Ernest Leonard Oulton and Henry Chadwick, *Alexandrian Christianity* [LCC; Philadelphia: Westminster, 1954] 43).

[16] *Acts Thom.* 129 (the translation comes from *NTApoc* 2. 511).

[17] Compare this phenomenon with the expansion of the images in the version of the tradition in the *Gospel of Thomas*: "the inside as the outside, and the outside as the inside, and the above as the below" (logion 22).

[18] Bartchy, *First-Century Slavery and 1 Corinthians 7:21* (SBLDS 11; Missoula: Scholars Press, 1973) 174.

[19] Attributed to Thales by Diogenes Laertius *Vitae philosophorum* 1.33; and to Plato by Lactantius *Divinae institutiones* 3.19 (cf. Plutarch, *Marius* 46.1).

thirdly, a Greek and not a barbarian.''[20] An inscription on a shrine at Philadelphia celebrates the overcoming of such social divisions in the cult of Agdistis:

> The commandments given to Dionysus, granting access in sleep to his own house both to free men and women, and to household slaves ... these commandments were placed [here] by Agdistis, the most holy Guardian and Mistress of this house, that she might show h r good will to men and women, bond and free.[21]

It would therefore seem likely that common awareness of these social polarities in the ancient world and Paul's own struggle against them in his mission suggested to him his alteration of the saying.

But perhaps we can be more precise concerning why Paul used these three pairs. They appear in an ancient Jewish prayer quoted by R.a Judah b. El'ai (ca. 150 CE) which Paul probably knew:

> There are three blessings one must pray daily:
> Blessed (art thou), who did not make me a gentile;
> Blessed (art thou), who did not make me a woman;
> Blessed (art thou), who did not make me an uncultured person.[22]

The Hebrew word *bôr*, here translated "uncultured person," could mean either a moron or someone destitute or uneducated. The Babylonian Talmud, however, repeats the same prayer but reads *'ebed*, or "slave," for *bôr*.[23] If this is the version of the prayer Paul knew, it would account for the presence of the same three pairs in Galatians; that is, Jew/gentile, man/woman, slave/free. The order of the last two pairs in Galatians might have been reversed owing to the male/female pair coming at the end of the Dominical Saying, or to Paul's seeing the slave as "the outside(r)" and the free person as "the inside(r)."

Dom. Saying	Gal 3:27–28	*t. Ber.*
When the two become one,	There is no Jew or Greek.	...who did not make me a Gentile.

[20] Diogenes Laertius *Vitae philosophorum* 1.33.
[21] F. C. Grant, *Hellenistic Religions* (Indianapolis: Bobbs-Merrill, 1953) 28–30.
[22] *t. Ber.* 7:18. Cf. *y. Ber.* 9:1. See also Raphael Loewe, *The Position of Women in Judaism* (London: SPCK, 1966) 42–44.
[23] *b. Menaḥ.* 43b.

| and the outside as the inside and the male with the female neither male nor female. | There is no slave or free.

There is no male and female. | ...who did not make me a woman.
...who did not make me a slave. |

Prior to baptism, the human community was polarized into Jews/Greeks, slaves/free, men/women. In baptism all become one.

In the interest of fairness it must be noted that several rabbinic texts also attempt to bridge these social poles.

> Before God ... all are equal: women, slaves, poor, and rich. (*Exod. Rab.* 21:4 [eleventh or twelfth century, ascribing the saying to two rabbis from the third and fourth centuries])[24]

> I call heaven and earth to witness that whether Gentile or Israelite, man or woman, slave or handmaid reads this verse ... the Holy One, blessed be He, remembers the binding of Isaac. (*Seder Eliahu* 7 [10th century])[25]

> Whether it be Israelite or Gentile, man or woman, slave or handmaid, whoever does a good deed shall find the reward. (*Yalkut Lek leka* 76 [12th century at the earliest])[26]

Notice, however, that the earliest of the parallels is later than Galatians by almost a century, and that all of them speak of equality only before God. None of them could be considered evidence for the breakdown of these barriers in historical experience.

4.5 There Is No . . .

Niederwimmer and Dautzenberg both argue that later tradition "eschatologized" Gal 3:28 or the saying it quotes. "There is no . . . " became "When. . . ." But surely they are wrong if by eschatology they mean the end of time or the state of the soul after death. The Dominical Saying refers not to the eschaton but to baptism. "When

---

[24] The translation comes from Madeleine Boucher, "Some Unexplored Parallels to 1 Cor 11:11–12 and Gal 3:28: The NT on the Role of Women," *CBQ* 31 (1969) 54.

[25] Ibid., 53.

[26] As translated in C. G. Montefiore and H. Loewe, *Rabbinic Anthology* (London: Macmillan, 1938) 380.

you tread upon the garment of shame" was realized in the discarding—and perhaps trampling—of the prebaptismal garment. "The two" were thought to have become one already in baptism. The issue then is not whether Christians in the second century "eschatologized" Gal 3:28 but whether they changed the mood and tense to express what initiates were about to experience in baptism.

Surely it is more likely that Paul "historicized" the Dominical Saying. It is reasonable to infer from the use of "when you . . ." that the saying was uttered to initiates prior to their baptisms. After baptism they could say, "We have trampled on the garment of shame, the two have become one, the outside has become as the inside, and the male with the female is no longer male and female." Such use of the past tense in fact appears over and over again in related texts. For example, in the *Acts of Thomas* a couple say they already have taken off "the garment of shame."[27] Apparently alluding to baptism, the *Odes of Solomon* says, "I took away from me my garments of skin" (25:8); "I put off darkness and put on light" (21:3). Thomas claims, "The inside I have made outside, and the outside 'inside'."[28]

I suggest, therefore, that the change in tense and mood from the aorist (a Greek past tense) subjunctive ("when you . . .") to the present indicative ("there is no . . .") may likewise be the result of Paul's looking back on baptism as a historical experience for all Christians. It is also possible, of course, that the change is more tendentious, either to indicate that the conditions articulated in the saying for seeing the kingdom of God already have been satisfied, or, if he had the Jewish blessing in mind, to indicate that the social divisions praised in the prayer had been abolished in baptism.

Conclusion

Paul's alterations of the Dominical Saying are consistent with his polemic against this same baptismal anthropology in 1 Corinthians. The initiate must put on Christ, not put off the flesh. Baptism is not a mystery rite insuring the initiate of oneness with God or with one's heavenly syzygy, but a symbol of social unity in Christ. The church

[27] *Acts Thom.* 14.
[28] Ibid., 147. So also Peter in the *Acts of Peter*, while hanging upside down, says he had fulfilled Jesus' command to "make what is on the right hand as what is on the left and what is on the left hand as what is on the right and what is above as what is below, and what is behind as what is before" (38).

is the new creation in which alienated social groups—Jews/Greek, slaves/free, men/women—were united. Perhaps Paul's list of social opposites was adopted from a Jewish prayer, in which case Paul would have suggested that God's new creation had broken down the very distinctions praised in the prayer.

Conversely, there is no consistent interpretive principle to explain how Gal 3:27–28 might have evolved into the Dominical Saying. Therefore, if there is any relationship between the two, the Dominical Saying is the more primitive.

The detailed analysis of the parallels provided in this chapter may suggest that Paul sat down with the Dominical Saying before him while he patiently crafted his own version. Oral tradition does not work so intentionally; neither, in all probability, did Paul. His alterations of the saying surely are simpler than may appear from our study, for each evolved from two fundamental convictions: (1) that the body must not be discarded, and (2) that the new creation must raze the walls protecting the privileged—whether Jews by dint of Torah obedience, or the "free" by dint of legal status, or men by dint of XX chromosomes—and excluding the disadvantaged—whether gentiles, slaves, or women.

CONCLUSION

5.1 The Trajectory of the Dominical Saying

By comparing Gal 3:26-28 with the Dominical Saying (Chapter 1), we have seen that the two passages are so structurally and verbally similar that some genetic relationship between the two is likely. Furthermore, by suggesting that Paul was dependent on this saying, one can account for the structural elements in Gal 3:26-28 which scholars have previously identified as indicating the presence of some tradition. We have also seen that the most likely performative setting for the Dominical Saying was baptism (Chapter 2), confirming our thesis that Paul was dependent on it, inasmuch as the reference to baptism seems gratuitous to his general argument in Galatians. In addition, Paul's alterations of the saying correspond with his opposition in 1 Corinthians to the anthropology and soteriology it presupposed (Chapters 3 and 4). It would appear that, like the preacher of *2 Clement* and Clement of Alexandria, Paul used the saying by shaping its malleable imagery for his own ends.

It should now be possible to trace the trajectory or history of the Dominical Saying. The precise origin of the saying itself still lies in the penumbral past, even though it was attributed to Jesus in the *Gospel of the Egyptians*, *2 Clement*, and the *Gospel of Thomas*. The anthropology and Genesis speculation implied by the saying were foreign to Jesus, but were quite at home in Alexandrian Judaism—for example, Philo—and in Corinthian Christianity by the time Paul wrote 1 Corinthians (53/54 CE). Perhaps these ideas were introduced in Corinth by Apollos, who like Philo was a Hellenistic Jewish

biblical scholar from Alexandria. He arrived in Corinth several years
before Paul wrote Galatians and 1 Corinthians. Whether or not
Apollos transmitted these ideas, the Corinthians shared with Philo
speculations on the first and second Adams, disdain for the body,
and hopes of a sacramental escape from the material world. Also,
the Corinthian women, like Asenath of the Hellenistic Jewish
romance, symbolized their return to the divine image by removing
their veils. It is likely, therefore, that the saying came from a Christian community influenced, as was Corinth, by Alexandrian Judaism.
Paul knew of the saying by the year 53 when he wrote Galatians.
He altered it so that putting off the garment of shame became putting on Christ, and the two sexes' becoming one became all social
groups' becoming one in Christ. These alterations suggest that for
Paul baptism was not the means by which the individual escaped the
body and was restored to the primordial state; rather, baptism was
the symbol by which the individual expressed membership in a new
creation, a unified community.

These alterations of the saying correspond to Paul's polemic in 1
Corinthians, written about two years after Galatians. Several times
Paul objected to the idea that the body must be put off; rather, believers must wait to put on the image of the heavenly Adam, Christ
(1 Cor 15:49; cf. vss 53-54). Paul also argued that baptism could not
assure one of moral or ontological perfection (1 Cor 10:1-12; 15:29);
after all, baptism was essentially a symbol of Christian unity (1 Cor
12:13).

Paul's interpretation of baptism did not prevail—not even in later
Pauline tradition. Colossians, written in the first century by someone apparently closely related to Paul, recast Gal 3:26-28 giving full
play to the imagery of putting off the old human and returning to the
divine image:

> Put off the old human with his deeds, and put on the new
> human renewed unto knowledge according to the image of the
> one who created him, where there is no Greek and Jew, circum-
> cised and uncircumcised, barbarian, Scythian, slave, free, but
> Christ is all things and in all things. (3:9-11)

Conspicuously absent is the pair male/female, presumably omitted
because the author of Colossians required women to be subject to
their husbands (3:18). Conspicuously present is the image of putting
off the old human, which the author of Colossians identified with
"putting off the body of flesh" (2:11). He says, as did Paul, "You
were buried with him in baptism," but he continues to say, as Paul

could not, "You were also raised with him through faith in the working of God who raised him from the dead" (2:12).

The author of Ephesians shares this conviction: "But God . . . made us alive together with Christ . . . and raised us up with him, and made us sit with him in the heavenly places" (1:4-6). Presumably, this exalted state results from baptism, for the author seems to be reminding his readers of their baptisms when he tells them to

> put off the old human which belongs to your former manner of life and is corrupt through deceitful lusts, and be renewed in the spirit of your minds, and put on the new human created after the likeness of God. (4:22-24)

Not even the textual tradition of the authentic Pauline letters was safe from the pens of those who believed in a baptismal resurrection. In Paul's name we find his opponents' sacramentology.

Furthermore, in spite of Paul's attempt to nip it in the bud, the Dominical Saying flourished in early Christian communities far removed from each other geographically and theologically. The preacher of *2 Clement* knew and used the saying, although he interpreted it in ways quite congenial to the "orthodox." The saying also found its way into the *Gospel of Thomas*, and informed the baptismal anthropology of Valentinians (esp. Julius Cassianus) and Syrian Christians. The *Exegesis on the Soul* (Valentinian) and the shorter text of the *Acts of Thomas* (Syrian) both show traces of just such baptismal symbolism. It is difficult to know how long this interpretation of baptism lasted, but there is reason to think it continued for at least a century after Clement of Alexandria rejected it in book three of the *Stromateis*. Both the *Gospel of the Egyptians* and the *Gospel of Thomas* were used until the fourth century; and celibate requirements for baptism continued in Syria to the death of Aphraates, and among some Gnostics and Marcionites until both were absorbed into the Manichaean movement, itself rigorously ascetic.

5.2 Sexual Division in Paul

This study has attempted to navigate safely between the Charybdis of supposing that Gal 3:26-28 is a verbatim quotation and the Scylla of supposing it is an ad hoc assertion of Paul's unique commitment to social equality "in Christ." Gal 3:26-28 is both traditional and original. If correct, this thesis requires a reassessment of the two dominant interpretations of the passage.

First, it is illegitimate to view Gal 3:26-28 as a testament to pre-Pauline social equality. "There is no male and female" is Paul's vision of sexual equality in his communities as they *should* be, not a witness to conditions in these communities as they were in fact. Paul's modifications of the Dominical Saying suggest he may have been more, not less, committed to sexual equality than was the tradition he opposed. At least he did not think women must become male to undo Eve's error.

On the other hand, it would be naive to presume that Paul's innovation in Gal 3:26-28 makes him a quondam feminist. Such a presumption surely commits chronological injustice, for it wrongly extradites Paul from his world and places him on trial in our own. We must allow him to return to the first century, and judge him in light of the problems and presuppositions of that age. When we do so, we can see more clearly the complexity of Paul's attitudes toward sexuality.

Paul did not write Gal 3:26-28 as a manifesto for sexual equality. The reference to male/female unity came from a traditional formula. Furthermore, this pair was the least important for Paul since he omitted it in 1 Cor 12:13 where he was no longer directly dependent on the Dominical Saying. Paul used the saying in Galatians to appeal for the unity of Jews and Greeks in Christ, an appeal he saw in the phrase "when the two become one." Paul was no feminist.

Likewise, it is unfair to single out Paul's reference to women's ontological inferiority in 1 Cor 11:2-16 as the epitome of his attitude on the subject. In this passage Paul opposed the now extinct practice of women taking off their veils in worship by which they symbolized their becoming male and returning to the divine image. In order to compensate for their inferiority to men and to demonstrate their participation too in the divine image, Paul tells women to wear their head coverings, not remove them as Corinthian practice had prescribed. To us, Paul's logic here is neither impressive nor necessary, but it may not have been for Paul himself. Immediately after saying women were derived from men and therefore inferior, he seems to reverse field, *"In the Lord* woman is not independent of man nor man of woman; for as woman was made from man, so man is now born of woman. And all things are from God." This is not far, of course, from Paul's statement in Gal 3:28 that "there is no male and female. For you all are one *in Christ Jesus."*

Perhaps some will object to my reclothing these texts in out-of-date theological garments, supposing that by doing so I have shrouded universal truths in the rags of historical particulars. Be assured: I have not wished to trivialize the pertinence of these texts to an inclusive religious anthropology. By saying that Paul's statements about male/female relations were conditioned by a now dead debate I do not mean to imply that his comments are irrelevant to modern struggles for sexual equality. Even though he used the saying in Galatians primarily to support the unity of Jews and Greeks, by including sexual equality in the pairs of opposites to be united in Christ he has inspired in subsequent Christian tradition innumerable quests for egalitarian communities. Paul's own failure to develop the implications of his vision in Gal 3:26-28 has not deterred his spiritual offspring from doing so.

Furthermore, he seems to have objected to the notion that women must become male to undo Eve's Fall. One finds this sexist view a salvation in the tradition's genesis among Hellenistic Jews (e.g., Philo and perhaps *Joseph and Asenath*), in its Corinthian manifestation (1 Cor 11:2-16), and in Valentinian and Thomas Christianity.[1] By opposing this anthropology with its misogyny and asceticism, Paul affirmed human sexuality—both female and male. Paul was no sexist.

But perhaps Paul's most important contribution to our own reflection on sexuality is his insistence that Christian existence is one of process, not one of perfection. Both in his use of the saying in Gal 3:26-28 and in his polemic in 1 Corinthians, Paul objected to those who claimed that they had already achieved the divine image. With the Corinthians he agreed that believers no longer wore the image of the earthly Adam, but he disagreed that they had already put on the image of the heavenly Adam. For Paul, that was to happen ultimately only after death or at the Parousia. Christian existence in the present was one of faith, anticipation, and love.

This pattern of "no longer . . . not yet" suggests that we too must be satisfied with being a community in process. Our communities of faith, like Paul's, are frequently broken and divisive; nonetheless, our vision, like Paul's, is one of wholeness and unity in Christ, and our hope, like Paul's, lies in the assurance that power is made perfect in weakness. This recognition of our limitations should preclude both male and female chauvinism, and should remind us that the

---

[1] Even though in Valentinianism this motif did not necessarily refer to the female gender (since the imagery is often used for the female soul becoming united with her heavenly syzygy), the imagery itself was certainly misogynistic—and not only to our ears. Even Tertullian, who himself was not above a sexist remark, recognized the sexist nature of the imagery among Valentinians (*Adv. Val.* 32.5).

struggle for a more loving and fully human community is a perpetual one.

Paul must return to his own world; nonetheless, he remains important for ours, even in our struggles for sexual equality. In Gal 3:26-28, he envisioned a fully democratized community. In 1 Corinthians, he affirmed the value of the body and sexuality. And in both, he has reminded us that our existence too—whether male or female—is imperfect, incomplete, and penultimate.